Children and Decent People

Children
AND
Decent
People

EDITED BY

Alvin L. Schorr

BASIC BOOKS, INC., *Publishers*

NEW YORK

© 1974 by Basic Books, Inc.
Library of Congress Catalog Card Number: 73–82894
SBN: 465–01041–5
Manufactured in the United States of America
DESIGNED BY IRVING PERKINS
74 75 76 77 78   10 9 8 7 6 5 4 3 2 1

For Wendy, my daughter,
avid, ardent, and far-ranging,
a child of her own generation,
her own self above all.
This book is for her.
Though different from her style,
she will understand the stubborn
necessity for search.

The Authors

DUANE F. ALEXANDER, M.D., is Special Assistant to the Scientific Director at the National Institute of Child Health and Human Development, Bethesda, Maryland.

ARTHUR C. EMLEN, PH.D., is Professor of Social Work, Portland State University, Oregon.

DAVID G. GIL, B.A., M.S.W., D.S.W., is Professor of Social Policy, Brandeis University, Waltham, Massachusetts.

GEORGE HOSHINO, A.M., D.S.W., is Professor at the School of Social Work, University of Minnesota at Twin Cities, Minnesota.

SHIRLEY JENKINS, PH.D., is Professor at Columbia University School of Social Work, New York.

CHARLES U. LOWE, M.D., is Scientific Director, National Institute of Child Health and Human Development, Bethesda, Maryland.

THOMAS E. NUTT is Assistant Professor, Department of Urban Studies and Planning, Massachusetts Institute of Technology, Cambridge, Massachusetts

MARTIN REIN, PH.D., is Professor, Department of Urban Studies and Planning, Massachusetts Institute of Technology, Cambridge, Massachusetts

MARGARET K. ROSENHEIM, J.D., is Professor, School of Social Service Administration, University of Chicago, Illinois.

ALVIN L. SCHORR is General Director of the Community Service Society of New York.

HEATHER WEISS is a Ph.D. candidate at the Harvard Graduate School of Education, Cambridge, Massachusetts.

Contents

Introduction

We are setting out in search of the reasons why so many children do badly in the United States. Such searches have for years been captured and made helpless by the view that we are a child-centered country. We lavish attention and worldly goods on our children in a way that Europeans still find remarkable. Our children emancipate themselves from family control very early. As young adults, they are more likely to be getting help from parents than giving it.

Still, these are internal family matters. As a public matter, Congress equably entertains the idea that a childless couple needs as much money as a couple with two children or a mother with three children. (That was the radical welfare reform that was.) When President Nixon came to office in 1969, he noted the disparity between spending $1,750 per capita on the aged and only $190 per capita on children. He promised to improve the share of children; yet it deteriorated in the following years. And, as the newspapers record every day, for lack of public provision millions of children go poorly schooled, poorly nurtured, and poorly supervised.

Historian Barbara Gutmann Rosenkrantz believes that a strain of hostility to children developed in our society at about the turn of the century. Earlier, children had demanded much, but were still an economic asset on the farm or at work. It was when family farming really began to give way and when family industry was supplanted that children lost utility. Keeping youths in school seemed attractive as much because it might occupy them as because the economy was going to require or reward it. In the end, advanced education does not seem greatly to have displaced or sublimated intergenerational conflict. All the while, the ongoing drive to emancipate women and the rise and resurgence of population planning have fed their quanta of hostility toward children into the atmosphere. (This is not to say that women should not be emancipated or population not planned, of course.)

Ambivalence about children—indulgence, to be sure, but resentment also—is evident if one looks about: The general anger at college youth and hippies; proposals to limit the income tax exemption to two children and no more; news photographs of antibusing demonstrators overturning and setting fire to a bus full of children. After conducting a five-year study of physical abuse of children, David Gil concluded that dramatic instances reflect "subtle and at times not so subtle [encouragement to] use a certain measure of physical force in rearing children. . . . This cultural tendency can be noted in child-rearing practices of most segments of American society." [1] So the abused children who horrify us are merely extreme examples of general behavior.

If anger and resentment at children are part of our feelings, we are not required to approach child care as if inadequacies are failures of resources or reason only. Inadequacy may represent a failure of purpose. Following an attempted jailbreak by young offenders in Paris some years ago, Jacques Prévert wrote a song that swept the city:

> Bandits, riff-raff, thieves, and scoundrels!
> The pack that hunts down children
> Is composed of decent people.

If it is the decent people who hunt down children, the problem lies deeper than one may have thought.

One has a choice of approaches to the problem. It might be interesting to conduct a sweeping inquiry into attitudes toward children over the years, and to ask what sociology can tell us about the institutions that structure our relationships with children. We have chosen instead to focus on children who are, in one way and another, in need. They are the children who are dependent, because they have lost their parents or because their parents are in trouble; the children who are themselves troubled or delinquent; children who are poor; and children who for some quite ordinary reason need day care or baby-sitting or the attention of a physician. It is a narrower but more critical inquiry. A trend to earlier or later emancipation of children might seem an academic matter, but a child who needs a doctor and does not see one calls for action. And children who need care spotlight our attitudes to children where these ought to be most generous.

Historically, explorations of the care of our children have focused on the number and kinds of needy children and on the number and quality of services they receive. The presumption is that we will supply whatever discrepancy we see. With the failure of such studies to command attention, let alone response, experts have turned to studying the efficiency of various methods of child care. (Argument about cost effectiveness goes back at least to the 1909 White House Conference on Dependent Children, which pointed out that parents care for children better and cheaper than anyone else.) In these studies or arguments, the presumption is that a limited sum of money will be spent on children, but that the spenders may be educated to do it more effectively.

If we are to entertain the notion that adequate provision for children is really not intended, however, a deeper inquiry is called for. Then one asks how we have organized the system that serves children, how it preserves equilibrium at an inadequate level of service, and how it protects decent people from guilt. The chapters that follow are intended to offer access to such questions.

One need not approach the problem without insights. One insight or, if one likes, hypothesis is that services to children are in the hands of a series of professionals—social workers, lawyers, teachers, doctors, and nurses—who come to define what needs to be done for children in terms of what they or their employing organizations are prepared to do. It is a common, and possibly ubiquitous, failing of professions. Thus, for example, child welfare is defined by the Child Welfare League of America as

. . . social work practice in providing social services to children and youths whose parents are unable or need help to carry their child-rearing responsibilities, or whose communities fail to provide the resources and protection that children and their families require.[2]

Given the identity of child welfare and professional practice, one may become captured by the method and overlook the problem. In that case, psychiatrists in residential treatment centers would not be responsible for all the sick children outside their walls, adoption workers would not be attending to starving children, and so forth.

The problem of professional blinders may be compounded if, in the way they are fundamentally structured, public programs concerned with children are devoted to a poor and meanly valued segment of the population. It is true that social workers have been accused of social climbing—of trying to devote themselves more to the middle classes. Nevertheless, child welfare workers have for many years been closeted with the poor, minorities, and otherwise disadvantaged. Then may they not come to accept scarcity as a way of life? May they come to overlook the fact that people with more money and education use other (and better?) services for their children than child welfare agencies? If so, can such compartmentalization be an accident, or does it serve a function? To put the matter plainly, are public services for children organized in a class-bound institution that serves a class function?

Shirley Jenkins undertook a broad survey of the clientele and history of the field; her findings are in Chapter 1. Other authors took responsibility for more detailed examination of particular fields of service to children—financial support, health care, family foster care—but each is trying to evaluate a whole system of care rather than some particular kind of agency. In other words, what range of alternatives do families consider for their children, and which families use which alternatives? The authors also try to evaluate the quality of services; it will become evident that the alternatives available may in turn determine quality.

Readers who would avoid disorientation should be at home with the special meaning of certain terms. Foster care is care by anyone other than parents—in institutions or in foster families. The latter is naturally called foster family care. Day care is care away from home during the working or waking hours, in day care *centers* or in foster *family* day care. Delinquent children have been charged with a crime or are threatened with being charged with one. Neglected children have failed, in the judgment of a court, to receive minimum parental care and protection. Dependent children are all the other children who may have competent or concerned parents who, because of illness or other reason, cannot care for them. Readers to whom these definitions have a ring of novelty should look at them once again and press on armed.

The tone of some of our authors is impatient; they are describing matters they have understood for some time. In other chapters, a scholarly tone makes impatience hard to discern; that shows good training. Without introducing drama, poor and sparse care for children will be apparent to the thoughtful reader. Drama would not be hard to display, but we are on the trail of practical questions that lie beneath and bring on desperation:

1. What are the parts of the system of services to children, and who are served well and poorly?
2. What determines how much or how little we do for children in this system?
3. How can it be that children are abused, or neglected, or starved, or exploited, and we do no better?

Clues that experts can provide are in the following chapters; a set of conclusions is in Chapter 8.

During the period when I was finishing work on this book, Richard M. Titmuss died in London. It is a mark of his influence that, besides myself, three of the authors represented here in one way and another took instruction from him. Although I cannot so early express my personal debt to him, if I am not mistaken three general points of view that he spent his life representing or exploring are recognizable in this book. They are, first, an emphasis on the distributive consequences of social policy; second, a stubborn belief in altruism as a motive power for social policy; and third, a preoccupation with how individuals fare in social policy, even to being led into apparent inconsistency. He would appreciate these ideas in the book, but he would also have little to say about them. His mind would turn to some point that needs strengthening or to ways to convert the conclusions into practical policy.

I gratefully acknowledge that work for the book was done in part under the auspices of the Center for Studies in Income Maintenance Policy at New York University, supported by The Rockefeller Brothers Fund and the Milbank Memorial Fund.

ALVIN L. SCHORR
New York City

INTRODUCTION xvii

NOTES

1. David G. Gil, *Violence Against Children* (Cambridge, Mass.: Harvard University Press, 1970), p. 134.
2. *Child Welfare as a Field of Social Work Practice* (New York City: Child Welfare League of America and U.S. Children's Bureau, 1959), p. 6.

Children and Decent People

1

Child Welfare as a Class System

SHIRLEY JENKINS

Children's needs are universal, but they are met in a selective way. According to *Profiles of Children,*[1] ten million children in the United States under 18 lived below the poverty line in 1969, including six million whites and four million blacks; seven million children under 14 were being raised in a household without a father; and over five and a half million children under 21 were in families receiving public assistance. No more than half the children in need of social services were receiving them. Infant mortality rates were higher than in 12 other major developed nations.

The purpose here, however, is not to document need. This has been done, and done well, in several recent studies, including *Poor Kids,* written by the editor of this book.[2] The central hypothesis is that the well-intentioned child welfare system has in fact functioned as a holding operation that has tended to perpetuate the status quo.

Traditionally the field of child welfare was established to provide social services that supplement or substitute for parental care and supervision. Many families cannot manage by themselves, and their needs reflect problems not directly child-related—such as poor housing, poverty, and adult mental illness. Therefore, child welfare also includes services that attempt to remedy the consequences of inadequate social institutions. Either way, one is providing a deficit service—compensation for a family deficit or compensation for a social deficit.

When society seeks to redress deprivation, programs are designed to meet the needs of the deprived. In most instances "deprived" is synonomous with "poor." Services tend to be designed for special groups, rather than for all children. Thus the field of child welfare is oriented toward pathology and deprivation, an orientation that in overt and subtle ways affects program development and planning. There is substantial evidence that programs for the poor often are poor programs. So a system such as child welfare, designed as part of the solution, can instead become part of the problem.

The hypothesis that the field of child welfare as a system reflects the ordering of social class and socioeconomic status implies that its mechanisms reinforce the present structure. In foster care, for example, the goal of the system is not upward mobility for the lower-class child, but typically the return of the child to the same milieu from which he came.

Although argument is not always strengthened by analogy, this characterization of the child welfare system may be better understood by comparison with public education. There is little doubt that at its inception public education in the United States was based on egalitarian principles and the idea of an open system with opportunity for advancement. Public education was to be the lever that would help the poor enrich their lives, enter the labor market, and compete with the more affluent. It has become obvious that the public schools alone cannot compensate for early family deprivation and segregation, but the dream of universal entitlement persists.

That dream has become the basis for significant court decisions in California, Texas, and New Jersey on school tax equality, an issue now left to states by Supreme Court decision.[3] The issue is whether dependence on local property taxes to finance public education may "invidiously discriminate" against the poor because the quality of a child's education depends on the wealth of the district in which he happens to live. In other words, is there universal entitlement not only to education, but also to equal educational opportunity? By analogy, is the dependent child entitled not only to care, but to optimal care?

Where there is a dichotomy in social welfare between public and voluntary agencies, practice tends to work against the public agency. Titmuss, for example, states: "Separate state systems for the poor, operating in the context of powerful private welfare markets, tend to become poor standard systems. Insofar as they are able to recruit at all for education, medical care and other services, they tend to recruit the worst rather than the best. . . ."[4]

The hypothesis about child welfare can of course be faulted by reference to individual children who have gained from the system; to the many dedicated workers who are concerned about outcome; and to the agencies and institutions with integrity and concern for children who work to help them grow and achieve. But a system cannot be understood in terms of individual cases—whether good or bad—but must be looked at in terms of its interactions with other broad institutions of society. This is a difficult task.

Discussion of specific aspects of child welfare will form the content for succeeding chapters. Primary attention here will be given to the selectivity issue, namely the question of the extent to which child welfare programs are programs for the poor. Three aspects will be discussed: historical antecedents, the nature of the client population, and legal considerations.

Citations on the historical antecedents of selectivity give evidence on the early treatment of dependent children. Discussion on the familial and socioeconomic backgrounds of the children relate to the question of who is served. Finally, reference to legal institutions as they affect child welfare suggest that there is a dual system that makes for differential treatment for poor children.

HISTORICAL ANTECEDENTS OF SELECTIVITY

The view that dependent children have been subject to differential treatment by the state is well supported by historical evidence. From the earliest colonial settlement, particular social policies were designed for dependent children that did not apply to children under parental care. A few examples follow.[5]

Regardless of familial ties or their own inclinations, dependent children were used to provide free labor and to populate colonial settlement. In the early seventeenth century, "Transportation of idle and needy children from crowded England to labor-starved Virginia was regarded not only as a boon to the Virginia planters but a service to King and country and a kindness to the children."[6]

In 1619 the Virginia Company requested the city of London to furnish 100 children to serve as apprentices, and then in 1620 they requested authority to coerce these children to be sent to Virginia where "under severe masters they may be brought to goodness."[7] Such authority was granted by the Privy Council, including the right to imprison, punish, and dispose of them, should there be disorder. In 1645 children from the Dutch Alm Houses or orphan asylums were trans-

ported by the West India Company, and there is evidence
that in 1645 the Burgermasters of Amsterdam sent a cargo of
poor children to Peter Stuyvesant at Fort New Amsterdam.[8]
Documents cite reports at James City in 1646 in which the
county commissioners were cautioned "not to take up any
children but from such parents who by reason of their poverty are disabled to maintain and educate them."[9] In Boston
in 1672 there were orders to families to "dispose of their several children . . . abroad for servants to serve by indenture
. . . which if they refused to do the Magistrate and Selectman
will take their said children from them. . . ."[10]

The practice of binding out neglected, poor, and orphan
children was widespread in the eighteenth century and had
its origins in English practice and law, including the Poor
Law of 1601. It served as a system of social control for homeless children and represented the most economical kind of social provision as well. Virginia statutes in 1748 stated that
". . . to prevent the evil consequence of neglect or inability
of poor people to bring up their children in an honest and or-
derly course of life—where any persons . . . shall be . . .
judged incapable of supporting and bringing up their child
. . . it shall be lawful for the churchwardens . . . to bind
every such child or children apprentices, in the same manner
. . . as the law directs for poor orphan children."[11]

If children who were bound out in New York City about
1800 were injured or ill-treated, the superintendent had the
duty of securing redress. It was noted, "They are to be
considered, in every respect, as the children of the public,
under his care."[12] As a matter of policy, orphan children and
poor children were treated in the same way, with poverty the
criterion for intervention in family affairs or removal of children from parents. The concept of "children of the public" is
also interesting, as many were children who had parents; the
lack of support resulted in abrogation of parental rights.

The situations of black children and immigrant children in the nineteenth century are also interesting. As now, the ethnic and social positions of children created special problems for them. Under slavery the black child was totally without rights. Not only was he without protection, but the slave family did not exist in a legal sense. Thus, slave owners could separate parents and children as they wished.

In a controversy concerning inheritance from a slave owner in South Carolina in 1809, the court decision held that the children of his slave should be distributed like the colts of his mare. Citing civil law on domestic animals, the court said, "This law applies to the young of slaves, because as objects of property, they stand on the same footing as other animals. . . ."[13] Emancipation proclamations tended to free the next generation of slaves rather than the present one. The Pennsylvania statute, for example, provided for bond servitude for the children of slaves until the age of 28.[14]

By the nineteenth century immigrant families constituted a new poverty group, and their children began to be regarded as a social problem. In 1853, for example, the New York Children's Society reported that "It is a fact worth noticing, that for all the many children who come under our operations, very seldom, indeed, is ever one an American or a Protestant."[15]

By the end of the nineteenth century, orphan asylums were the prevalent way of providing institutional care to dependent children, although the use of foster homes for homeless street children was encouraged. Controversy about the merits of foster homes versus institutions was widespread in the late nineteenth century. The issue of home care of children was thoroughly discussed at the 1909 White House Conference. The deliberations pointed both to home relief and foster care. The proceedings stated, "Except in unusual circumstances, the home should not be broken up for reasons of poverty, but only for considerations of inefficiency or immorality." [16] Furthermore, when children had to be removed from their own homes, or if they had no homes, care in a foster home was considered to be the best substitute for the natural home.

A major milestone in the approach to child welfare was the establishment of the Children's Bureau in 1912, within the Department of Commerce and Labor, with the charge to investigate and report on "all matters pertaining to the welfare of children and child life among all classes of our people. . . ." [17] The critical phrase was "all classes of our people," a significant move to assert a national interest in all children, rather than only children considered to be dependent, neglected, or delinquent.

Although, from the beginning, the program of the Children's Bureau reflected concern for all children, findings from early investigations quickly directed their attention to poverty areas. The first report of the bureau was a study of infant mortality; one conclusion was that death rates of babies went down as fathers' earnings went up.[18] Julia C. Lathrop, chief of the Children's Bureau, said in 1919, "Children are not safe and happy if their parents are miserable, and parents must be miserable if they cannot protect a home against poverty. Let us not deceive ourselves: the power to maintain a decent family living standard is a primary essential of child welfare." [19]

These illustrations of the historical antecedents of our system of child care demonstrate that social policy has been different for dependent children and children reared by self-supporting parents—a different game played by different rules. In early years, many pauper children were abducted and bound in servitude. Later they were placed in special institutions, then often in substitute homes. But as a group their deprivation remains, and although they are "children of the public," they are not cherished by the state as a parent cherishes his own child.

THE CHILD CLIENT

Who are the current "children of the public," the recipients of child welfare? What do we know of their backgrounds or origins? By various program definitions, they may be under 14, 16, 18, 21, or 22 years. However, their age is about the only piece of hard data available when one attempts to describe these child clients as a group. There are several reasons for this paucity of information: the organization of child welfare services into national, state, and local levels; the involvement of both private and public agencies; the often indeterminate boundaries between family welfare and child welfare; the aversion of the social welfare field to the concept of a data bank, in which dossiers would be maintained on the poor, and the lag in introduction of modern information systems. All this means that there is no unified data collection, no centralized reporting, and no common data analysis. In particular, an unduplicated count of recipients is not available.

In order to describe the child client in socioeconomic terms, it is necessary to piece together information from disparate sources. Sometimes the information is aggregated from estimates based on individual studies, and sometimes it is inferred, such as when socioeconomic level is related to neighborhood, ethnic group, or other contextual data. The attempt is to assemble information to examine the hypothesis that child welfare is a selective system to serve the poor.

In a universal system, potential beneficiaries would presumably encompass the total child population, which in 1970 comprised 76,970,400 persons 19 years of age and under.[20] Under the present organization of services, the entitled population varies program by program. Figures on actual recipients show the estimated range of children affected.

If child welfare is broadly interpreted, income maintenance

programs under social insurance need to be considered. The largest of these provides social security payments to children of retired, deceased, or disabled parents. This program reached 4,123,327 child recipients under 21 in 1970.[21] This is a universal program, with benefits widely dispersed. The largest public assistance program for children is Aid to Families with Dependent Children (AFDC), which supported 7,389,677 youngsters during July 1971.[22] Some of these children may be receiving social security benefits as well, but by and large these two programs reach different populations. The socioeconomic and familial background of these seven million children is well known—they are living below the poverty level and are primarily from single-parent families. Children from minority groups are strongly overrepresented.

Moving from financial support to child services, the Children's Bureau estimated that 859,000 children were receiving child welfare services from both public and voluntary agencies in 1969.[23] About 75 percent were served by public agencies only, 19 percent by voluntary agencies only, and 6 percent by both. Services went approximately equally to youngsters in their own homes and in substitute care.

More is known about the background of children in foster care. For example, the Child Welfare League rated 1,200 families requesting foster care in seven metropolitan areas. Sixteen percent of families were in Classes I (highest) through III, 30 percent in Class IV, and 54 percent in Class V (lowest). Median gross family income of the families was about $73 a week, with public assistance providing support for 21 percent of the children.[24] A study in four other cities found that the more disadvantaged families more often had their children actually placed in foster homes. Their income was lower (58 percent under $100 a week), and they were more likely to be receiving public assistance than were families that asked for placement but did not carry through.[25]

Two studies with substantial samples in New York are in accord with these findings.[26] The large majority of the children were from one-parent households, half were supported by public assistance payments, and families with a worker had average weekly earnings of between $75 and $80. A Philadelphia study that includes families receiving services in their own homes reports comparable family circumstances.[27]

Children enter placement for a variety of reasons. A national survey of a decade ago reported that the single most important problem bringing children into care is neglect, abuse, or exploitation by parents or other persons responsible for the children.[28] There is some evidence on family background of such children. From an analysis of neglect complaints in Minneapolis and St. Paul: "The preponderance of the families referred for neglect come from the lower socio-economic strata of the community and differ markedly from the general population in education, income, neighborhood, race, and family structure. . . ."[29] For example, 42 percent of these neglect families were supported by public assistance, as compared with 3 percent of the total population; the percent of nonwhites in the neglect group was three times that in the general population.

A national study of physical child abuse in 1967 and 1968 reports that "The income of the families in the sample cohort was very low compared to the income of all families in the United States." In 1969, 48 percent of these abusive families had incomes under $5,000, as compared with 25 percent of all families in the United States. Furthermore, approximately 60 percent of abusive families had received aid from public assistance agencies during, or prior to, the study year.[30] Similarly, in New York City in 1971, of 52 deaths officially attributed to child abuse, 31 were in families on welfare.[31]

A census of children's residential institutions in 1966 reported 155,905 children and youths in 2,318 institutions.

One-third of the institutions were public and two-thirds private, but each group housed about half of the children, an indication of the larger capacity of public facilities. Of the children, 60,459 were in institutions for the dependent and neglected, 55,000 in institutions for delinquents and predelinquents, and 13,876 in institutions for the emotionally disturbed.[32] The seven-volume study gives no information on family, ethnic, or socioeconomic background.[33] An earlier study based on 1960 census data, shows that nonwhite children are more likely to wind up in an institution. Nonwhite children, only 13 percent of the national population, made up 33 percent of children in correctional institutions, 40 percent of children in tuberculosis hospitals, and 33 percent of children in hospitals for chronic diseases.[34]

In 1966 it was estimated that 473,800 children were receiving psychiatric treatment in the United States, of whom 399,-000 were attending outpatient psychiatric clinics.[35] In 1963, the Manhattan Society for Mental Health attempted to cast some light on the background of children receiving outpatient psychiatric services.[36] The study showed that the children of the poor, especially the "poorest poor," received proportionately less service than other children. Only 14 percent of children seen in outpatient clinics were in fact treated; the bulk of the clinics' work was diagnostic. In general, voluntary agencies were providing treatment services to children who were not poor; the public system was dealing with poorer children and doing little more than diagnosis.

Adoption is perhaps the most obscure children's service in terms of available information. About 171,000 children were adopted in the United States in 1969, slightly more than one-half by unrelated persons and the rest by relatives.[37] Two-thirds of the children were born out of wedlock, such births comprising nearly 90 percent of adoptions by nonrelatives. Black children constituted only 11 percent of all adopted children. It may be surmised that children who are adopted come from poorer homes and enter more middle-class homes. Adoption agencies generally require that prospective adoptive parents have at least a regular income. There is some indication, however, that mothers who surrender children may not be the most extremely deprived.

The Child Welfare League study that examined requests for substitute care found that mothers of children born out of wedlock and unwed mothers were better educated, represented more white-color occupations rather than blue-collar ones, and were generally higher in socioeconomic level than parents seeking other child welfare services.[38] The predominance of white adoptions also shows that adoption is not generally a route for the most socially deprived.

As for day care, in 1970 there were 16,600 licensed centers with a capacity of 625,800 children. Fewer than half of these were nonprofit (including 1,200 under public auspices) and the majority was proprietary. About 54 percent of children were in profit-making centers, and 46 percent in nonprofit ones.[39]

Working mothers are by far the major clientele of both proprietary and nonprofit centers. Of the proprietary centers, over 40 percent care only for children of working mothers; in another 40 percent, over 75 percent of the children have working mothers. In about half the centers most of the families are in the $5,000 to $10,000 income bracket. In only about 20 percent of the centers is family income for the majority less than $5,000 a year.

Of the nonprofit centers, over half care only for children of working mothers; in another one-third of these centers, children of working mothers comprise over 75 percent of enrollees. The lowest concentration of children of working mothers is found in the Head Start programs, where day care is often made necessary by other pressing circumstances, such as parental illness. In over two-thirds of the nonprofit centers, children with a single parent represent over 75 percent of enrollees. This is a striking difference from proprietary centers. Another key difference is in income level. Two-thirds of nonprofit centers cater primarily to very low income families (under $5,000), compared with only one-fifth of the proprietary centers. Not surprisingly, then, three-fourths of the proprietary centers serve predominantly white children. In 56 percent of the nonprofit centers, the majority of the children are black, and in 5 percent more the majority are of Puerto Rican or other Spanish-American heritage. In 89 percent of the Head Start centers, the majority of children are black.

Thus, children in nonprofit centers tend to be from poor, single-parent families—with mothers working or not—and those in proprietary centers are generally from poor or lower-middle-class, intact families.

The data presented are fragmentary and are based on varied sources, because of the lack of systematic information on family background of children receiving services. What is known, however, indicates that the large majority of children served in what are commonly known as child welfare agencies appear to be poor; it is a massive welfare system for children. Do the basic legal institutions reflect this?

IN LOCO PARENTIS

When the state assumes parental responsibility and acts "in loco parentis," juvenile and family courts interpret the law. Are dependent children treated differentially according to family circumstances?

Jacobus tenBroek has argued that a dual system of family

law is reflected in welfare policies—one law for the poor and
one for the nonpoor.[40] His studies of California law indicate
that conduct is regulated according to class. The handling of
neglected children, adoption, child custody, parental rights,
and delinquency reflect the family's economic status. Service
delivery in turn reflects legal interpretation.

A full exposition of the law in relation to needy children is
beyond the scope of this survey chapter. (Chapter 7 is devoted to the development and operation of juvenile and family courts.) However, a few issues will be raised to show that,
in relation to poor children, justice may be not blind, but otherwise handicapped.

For example, Herma Hill Kay and Irving Philips assert
that custody decisions are influenced by poverty. Moreover, it
is poverty itself that gives rise to the need for such decisions.[41] Furthermore, the financially independent mother has
more latitude in establishing her household than the applicant for public assistance. The latter must think of welfare
law, which may be far more prescriptive about her relationships than family law would be.

A major reason for removal of children from their homes is
a determination of neglect: in these situations poverty is often
the antecedent condition. The consequences of a dual system
of law for poor and nonpoor are often accentuated by related
social class biases. This is a double-edged sword, however.
For example, too ready acceptance of lower expectations of
family functioning in the case of the poor can lead to a double
standard, as well as to a dual system. A level of living may be
accepted as appropriate for a poor child that would not be
approved for the middle-class child. In such cases a clear differentiation should be made between those patterns that reflect merely cultural differences, as contrasted to conditions
that would in fact endanger the health and safety of the children involved.

In addition to problems raised about duality of law, the

poor child is often subjected to harsh treatment in the course of determination of legal decisions. Children in trouble with the law are in double jeopardy in that they are strictly speaking outside the protection of the child welfare system, but also typically excluded from legal protections afforded adults. The use of the *parens patriae* doctrine means that the child can be held "no matter how inadequate the place of detention or the type of care given." [42] In 1965 over 409,000 children were admitted to detention facilities and were held for an average of 12 days awaiting disposition. Although the Supreme Court decision *In re Gault* was followed by a move to strengthen legal protection for juveniles, the issue will not be resolved until community services are adequate to the needs of these youngsters.

In discussing the corrections system, the National Council on Crime and Delinquency concludes:

Confusion and misuse pervade detention. It has come to be used by police and probation officers as a disposition, judges use it for punishment, protection, storage, and lack of other facilities. More than in any other phase of the correctional process the use of detention is colored by rationalization, duplicity, and double talk. . . .[43]

Justine Wise Polier, an eminent judge in the family court in New York City, has commented that juvenile or family courts, presumably developed to strengthen family life, "have been treated as low man on the judicial totem pole, not requiring legal acumen, and have been starved for necessary administrative, judicial and service personnel." She adds, "For many thousands of children the gap between legislative purposes and judicial action spells a substantial denial of legal rights that demands reform far beyond the assurance of a fair trial." [44]

The problems of the family court have also been described by Monrad G. Paulsen, who concludes:

The fact that those who go to a juvenile court are generally the poor (in the big cities at least) transforms the court into a class institution, a fact which may inhibit its development and, indeed, may have an impact on all sorts of legislative choices. . . .[45]

The potential for differential treatment by courts is shaped not only by parental resources, but in turn by patterns of agency care. In New York State, children found delinquent or in need of supervision [46] may be dealt with in several different ways. They may be placed in a voluntary child care agency, they may be placed in a state training school, or they may be maintained in city shelters pending long-term placement or return to their homes. A survey of the pattern of disposition led to the following conclusion:

The picture drawn from the case sampling reveals serious discrimination. We found that voluntary agencies tend to discriminate against Black and Puerto Rican children, thus forcing the Court to place 76 per cent of the Black and 66 per cent of the Puerto Rican children in training schools and public shelters. In sharp contrast, 78 per cent of the White children are provided care by private, publicly funded agencies.

We found discrimination by voluntary agencies against children who lack "cooperative" families. We found discrimination against children with the most serious emotional problems, low IQ levels, and low reading levels. We found discrimination against children who are seriously involved with drugs, and we found discrimination against adolescents.[47]

CHILD WELFARE—
SELECTIVE SYSTEM?

Is child welfare a system that selects poor children? This chapter has raised the question and discussed three relevant background areas. Historical material shows that orphan and dependent children were from early times subject to state authority in quite a different way from other children. Current child welfare policies do not stem from a universal child-centered orientation, as is often assumed, but from a broad social tradition that separated the poor and dependent population from the rest of society.

Although national data on the background of child welfare recipients are limited, a range of sources indicate that it is primarily the poor child who is served. The excursion into legal issues indicates that there is a special family law for poor children—the "law of the poor." The distinction applies both in decisions and in execution of court orders.

That a separate system for the care of poor children may result in poor care is not a new idea. In 1938, Grace Abbott wrote:

For those children who are wholly dependent upon the state, or especially handicapped by reason of birth or physical or mental defect, who are becoming delinquent or are delinquent, the state has a special responsibility.

Speaking of education, John Dewey said, "What the best and wisest parent wants for his own child, that must the community want for all of its children. . . ."

In its provision for the children in need of special care the state has, however, not acted on Mr. Dewey's theory. Generally speaking, it has undertaken to provide for their care only when the evidence of need made such action inevitable. Reluctant to undertake a clear duty, it is not surprising that legislatures have sought to provide not "what the best and wisest parent wants for his own child" but the cheapest possible care, and that law-makers have been slow to recognize that this not only violated sound humanitarian tenets but was in the long run very costly economy.[48]

A new frame of reference is needed to move child welfare from selective application into the broader arena of universal services. As we examine child welfare services for the poor, we may well ask, how do those who are not poor approach and solve the same problems for their children? Where do they turn for help? Also, what are the problems that simply do not arise unless one is poor? The answers to these questions may provide some clues to the inequities resulting from the duality of the present system and, more importantly, point to new goals and directions for child welfare.

NOTES

1. *Profiles of Children,* 1970 White House Conference on Children (Washington, D.C.: Government Printing Office), pp. 19, 22, 24, 25, 47.
2. Alvin L. Schorr, *Poor Kids* (New York: Basic Books, 1966).
3. *New York Times,* January 10, 1972, Annual Education Review, pp. 1E, 26E. Also, see *New York Times,* April 9, 1973, editorial, "Warning to the States," p. 36.
4. Richard M. Titmuss, "Choice and the Welfare State," in *Commitment to Welfare* (New York: Pantheon Books, 1968), p. 143.
5. Robert H. Bremner, ed., *Children and Youth in America, A Documentary History, Vol. 1, 1600–1865* (Cambridge, Mass.: Harvard University Press, 1970) is a valuable source of information on this earlier period. Historical references that follow are taken from its compendium of original records, documents, legal papers, and communications of the time.
6. Bremner, *Children and Youth in America, Vol. 1,* p. 6.
7. Bremner, *Children and Youth in America, Vol 1,* pp. 7, 8.
8. Bremner, *Children and Youth in America, Vol. 1,* p. 23.
9. Bremner, *Children and Youth in America, Vol. 1,* pp. 65–66.
10. Bremner, *Children and Youth in America, Vol. 1,* p. 69.
11. Bremner, *Children and Youth in America, Vol. 1,* p. 263.
12. Bremner, *Children and Youth in America, Vol. 1,* p. 276.
13. Bremner, *Children and Youth in America, Vol. 1,* pp. 330–331.
14. Bremner, *Children and Youth in America, Vol. 1,* pp. 324–325.
15. Bremner, *Children and Youth in America, Vol. 1,* p. 416.
16. Bremner, *Children and Youth in America, A Documentary History, Vol. 2, 1866–1932,* p. 365.

17. Bremner, *Children and Youth in America, Vol. 2*, p. 774. The Children's Bureau has undergone various administrative shifts. In 1946, minus its child labor functions, it was transferred to the Federal Security Agency which, by Act of Congress, became in 1953 the Department of Health, Education, and Welfare. In 1972, the Children's Bureau was incorporated into the Office of Child Development in the same department. (See *Children Today*, U.S. Department of Health, Education, and Welfare, vol. 1, no. 2, Anniversary Issue, Children's Bureau, 1912–1972, March–April 1972.)

18. Dorothy E. Bradbury, *Five Decades of Action for Children*, U.S. Department of Health, Education, and Welfare, Children's Bureau (Washington, D.C.: Government Printing Office, 1962), pp. 6–7.

19. Bradbury, *Five Decades of Action for Children*, p. 8.

20. U.S. Bureau of the Census, *Census of Population: 1970, General Population Characteristics, Final Report PC(1)–B1 United States Summary* (Washington, D.C.: Government Printing Office, 1972), p. 276.

21. *Social Security Bulletin*, 34, no. 12 (December 1971), 69. This total includes 537,297 students from 18 to 21, and 270,609 persons who had disabilities arising in childhood.

22. *Social Security Bulletin*, 34, no. 12 (December 1971), 56.

23. *Child Welfare Statistics, 1969*, U.S. Department of Health, Education, and Welfare, Social and Rehabilitation Service, pp. 1–2, 21. Kinds of services included are primarily public and voluntary foster care in foster families and child welfare institutions, homemaker services, and day care under child welfare, but not public assistance, auspices.

24. Ann W. Shyne, *The Need for Foster Care, An Incidence Study of Requests for Foster Care and Agency Response to Seven Metropolitan Areas* (New York: Child Welfare League of America, 1969), pp. 40–41.

25. Michael H. Phillips, Ann W. Shyne, Edmund A. Sherman, and Barbara L. Haring, *Factors Associated with Placement Decisions in Child Welfare* (New York: Child Welfare League of America, 1971), pp. 22–23.

26. Shirley Jenkins and Mignon Sauber, *Paths to Child Placement* (New York: Community Council of Greater New York, 1966), pp. 40–47; Shirley Jenkins and Elaine Norman, "Families of Children in Foster Care," *Children*, 16, no. 4 (July–August 1969) 155–156.

27. Joseph L. Taylor, "The Child Welfare Agency as the Extended Family," *Child Welfare*, 51, no. 2 (February 1972), 74.

28. Helen R. Jeter, *Children Problems and Services in Child Welfare Programs,* U.S. Department of Health, Education, and Welfare, Children's Bureau (Washington, D.C.: Government Printing Office, 1963), pp. 14–24.
29. Bernice Boehm, "The Community and the Social Agency Define Neglect," *Child Welfare,* 43, no. 9 (November 1964), 459.
30. David G. Gil, *Violence Against Children, Physical Child Abuse in the United States* (Cambridge, Mass.: Harvard University Press, 1970), p. 112.
31. *New York Times,* February 14, 1972.
32. Donnell M. Pappenfort, Dee Morgan Kilpatrick, and Alma M. Kuby, *A Census of Children's Residential Institutions in the United States, Puerto Rico, and the Virgin Islands: 1966, Vol. 1* (Chicago: The University of Chicago, The School of Social Service Administration, Social Service Monographs, 2d ser., 1970), p. 19.
33. On this point, it has been argued that color is identified when counting problems, to be sure, but not when counting services. See Andrew Billingsley and Jeanne M. Giovannoni, *Children of the Storm, Black Children and American Child Welfare* (New York: Harcourt Brace Jovanovich, 1972).
34. Seth Low, *America's Children and Youth in Institutions 1950–1960–1964,* U.S. Department of Health, Education, and Welfare, Children's Bureau (Washington, D.C.: Government Printing Office, 1965), pp. 8–10.
35. *Crisis in Child Mental Health: Challenge for the 1970's,* Report of the Joint Commission on Mental Health of Children (New York: Harper & Row, 1969), p. 268.
36. Sylvan S. Furman, Lili G. Sweat, and Guido M. Crocetti, "Social Class Factors in the Flow of Children to Outpatient Psychiatric Facilities," *American Journal of Public Health,* March 1965, pp. 385–392.
37. *Adoptions in 1969, Supplement to Child Welfare Statistics—1969,* U.S. Department of Health, Education, and Welfare, National Center for Social Statistics (Washington, D.C., 1971).
38. Ann W. Shyne, *The Need for Foster Care,* pp. 38–40.
39. Mary Dublin Keyserling, *Windows on Day Care* (New York: National Council of Jewish Women, 1972). Data on day care are taken from chaps. 4 and 5, pp. 40–129. There is no national survey of the family background of children in day care. The information in the text here is generalized to the degree that seems reasonable from *Windows on Day Care.*
40. Jacobus tenBroek and the editors of *California Law Review,* eds., *The Law of the Poor* (San Francisco, Chandler Publishing Co., 1966).

41. Herma Hill Kay and Irving Philips, "Poverty and the Law of Child Custody," in *The Law of the Poor*, ed. tenBroek, pp. 393–416.

42. The President's Commission on Law Enforcement and Administration of Justice, *Task Force Report: Corrections*, Appendix A, The National Council on Crime and Delinquency, *Corrections in the United States*, p. 119.

43. *Corrections in the United States*, p. 121.

44. Justine Wise Polier, "The Invisible Legal Rights of the Poor," *Children*, 12, no. 6 (November–December 1965), 215–216.

45. Monrad G. Paulsen, "Juvenile Courts, Family Courts, and the Poor Man," in *The Law of the Poor*, ed. tenBroek, p. 373.

46. A juvenile delinquent is a child between the ages of 7 and 16 who is found to have committed an act that is a crime when committed by an adult. A "person in need of supervision" is a boy under the age of 16 or a girl under the age of 18 found to be incorrigible, out of control of lawful authority, or a habitual truant.

47. *Juvenile Justice Confounded: Pretensions and Realities of Treatment Services*, Committee on Mental Health Services Inside and Outside the Family Court in the City of New York, National Council on Crime and Delinquency, 1972, pp. 22–23.

48. Grace Abbott, *The Child and the State*, vol. 2 (Chicago: University of Chicago Press, 1938), pp. 611–612. The quotation Abbott cites is from John Dewey, *The School and Society* (Chicago: University of Chicago Press, 1899), p. 3.

2

Foster Family Care: Myth and Reality

MARTIN REIN, THOMAS E. NUTT, AND HEATHER WEISS

INTRODUCTION

Contemporary literature attests to a consistent, temperate, and scholarly stream of criticism of the foster family care system over the last 15 years or more. This literature stands as well as a testament to its ineffectiveness in contributing to any important demonstrable changes. Rather than add yet another critical article, we are in search of a different point of view that may help in understanding the stubborn resistance to significant changes.

Our main thesis is that a good part of the stability and dysfunction in foster family care lies in the system's class biases. In foster care, middle-class professionals provide and control a service used mostly by poor people, with upper-lower-class and lower-middle-class foster parents serving as intermediaries. Their biases control the goals of the system, its boundaries, and the quality of care. A careful review of available data reveals several important paradoxes. For example, though foster care appears to place a premium on the nuclear family, it does little to enable the child to return to his own home or some other more or less permanent one. The result is that foster care becomes a trap for many, and one to which a good deal of stigma attaches.

There is a different pattern of substitute care for the non-poor, such as private boarding schools or care by relatives. Part of the larger system (but not reviewed in this chapter) are services that quite avoid the need for foster family care: day care, psychiatric treatment, maids, day schools. These provisions render a different standard of care, often without public intervention and stigma. One function of two separate systems is to maintain a view that the need for substitute care arises in the first place from the child's inadequacy or his family's. A second function is to legitimize the allocation to poor children of services that are inferior in quantity or quality. These class biases operate to stabilize the present system of foster family care. Studies of attitudes and practices conclude that, "Although a wide variety of such changes aimed at improving the quality of services were reported as taking place, the adoption of accepted standards and established procedures cannot be termed innovative." [1] It seems unlikely that pressure for major changes will arise within the foster care system itself.

FOSTER CARE AS A CLASS-BOUND SYSTEM: THE EVIDENCE

The nuclear family is assumed to be prerequisite for proper child development. A home without natural parents is regarded as "substitute care" with the strong presumption that it should be only a temporary condition. Yet in March of 1970 some 2,378,000 children under 18 years of age were living with neither natural parent or in no family at all.[2] This represented 4.4 percent of all children under 18 years of age. Only 20 percent of this number were receiving services from a child welfare agency (see Table 2–1). Little systematic attention has been given to the other 80 percent of children in substitute care.

There are two basic sources of information on these populations—the Census Bureau and the National Center for Social Statistics at the Department of Health, Education, and Welfare. It is of doubtful validity to compare these data sources because of basic differences in the definitions used and other limitations of published data. Agencies actually involved in foster care provide little that is more penetrating.

TABLE 2–1

Children Receiving Child Welfare Services, March 1970

| | AUSPICES | | | |
Living Arrangement	Public	Public and Voluntary	Voluntary	Estimated Unduplicated Total
In homes of relatives	115,000	—	3,100	118,100
In independent living arrangements	10,500	—	4,800	15,300
Foster family homes	217,000	25,600	15,800	258,400
Group homes	2,200	1,400	1,100	4,700
Child welfare institutions	7,000	30,300	25,300	62,600
Maternity homes	—	2,300	3,200	5,500
Elsewhere	8,000	—	2,100	10,100
Total	359,700	59,600	56,400	475,700

SOURCE: U.S. Department of Health, Education, and Welfare, National Center for Social Statistics "Children Served by Public Welfare Agencies and Voluntary Child Welfare Agencies and Institutions—March 1970," March 10, 1972, abstracted from Tables 1, 5, 7.

For example, Stone's 1969 survey among agencies of the Child Welfare League of America found that 43 percent of the respondents could not specify the number of children coming into their care on an emergency basis.[3] With regard to evaluation, 73 percent of the respondents were not conducting any studies of children currently under care; 87 percent were not doing any postdischarge or follow-up studies.[4]

Substitute care appears to be widely distributed among social classes. The 1,593,000 children in substitute family care [5] include both rich and poor children living with aunts, uncles, brothers, sisters, grandparents, friends, or in foster families or group homes. The remaining 785,000 children not living with families [6] reside in a wide range of places, including for example state training schools.

Limiting our analysis to children living outside the nuclear family understates the effect of certain kinds of substitute care, such as nursery school or day care, homemaker services or baby-sitting exchanges. For example, a study of child care arrangements in Massachusetts reports that parents of preschool children are more likely to be regularly away from home, if they have higher incomes.[7] One-third of all preschool children in Massachusetts regularly spend time in a kindergarten or similar arrangement, and almost all children whose family income is above $15,000 make use of some form of temporary substitute care. In general, then, short-term substitute care is widely utilized.

By contrast, the substitute care population that receives what official statistics call "child welfare services" is disproportionately lower class, lower income, and nonwhite. For example, the Child Welfare Research Program at Columbia University concluded, "Just prior to being placed in foster care, the majority of children in the study lived in impoverished households located in the poorest of neighborhoods of New York City." [8] A 1969 Child Welfare League of America study provides the most complete picture of the official foster care population; [9] relevant data are summarized in Table 2–2. All but 16 percent of the families were either Class IV or V (Class I is the highest, V the lowest). Nearly three-fourths of the requests came from families with annual incomes of $4,800 or less (1966 incomes); about one-fourth received AFDC or some other form of public assistance; one-fifth were nonwhite; one-fifth of the fathers were unemployed; only

TABLE 2–2

Characteristics of Parents of Foster Children

	Percent of Families	Percent of Mothers	Percent of Fathers
Race			
White		80	81
Nonwhite		20	19
High school graduate		50	53
Employed (full time or part time)		35	81
White-collar occupation		39	30
Socioeconomic status			
Class I, II, III	16		
Class IV	30		
Class V	54		
Monthly income (1966)			
Under $200	22		
$200–$399	50		
$400 and over	29		
Public assistance status			
AFDC °	17		
Other public assistance	7		
None	77		

SOURCE: Ann W. Shyne, *The Need for Foster Care, An Incidence Study of Requests for Foster Care and Agency Response in Seven Metropolitan Areas* (New York: Child Welfare League of America, 1969), abstracted from Tables IV–3, V–4, V–5, V–6. Used by permission.
° Aid to Families with Dependent Children. Alone or in combination with other public assistance.

one-third had white-collar occupations; and only one-half
were high school graduates.

The 1966 Jenkins and Sauber study provides data on the
family's source of income support at the time a child came
into foster care. They found that "the source from which the
largest number of families derived income was . . . the Department of Welfare, which was the major support for 38%
of the families. An almost equal proportion, comprising
34% of all families, was self-supporting. The remainder
lived primarily on savings, benefit and other payments, or
help from friends or relatives." [10] They also found that only
16 percent of white families, but about 45 percent each of
black and Puerto Rican families derived their main source of
support from public assistance.[11]

Middle-income families make use of a limited sector of the
official foster care system; they do so for specific reasons. Jenkins and Sauber explain that:

The cost of treatment and residential placement for disturbed children . . . is so high that the average middle-class, self-supporting
family, which might never have had contact with the Department
of Welfare in any other context, cannot manage to undertake this
burden for any substantial period of time without the assistance of
some public funds.[12]

Shyne's data showed that only 16 percent of the children fell
into Classes I, II, or III.[13] The primary reason that foster or
institutional care was asked for these children was that they
were born out of wedlock.

The Origin of Class Bias in Foster Care

The class-bound nature of the official foster care system is
the consequence of both history and current professional
practice in the field. Presumably, professional practice is

geared to assist all social classes in an essentially objective, value-free manner. In fact, both practice and the assumptions and standards on which practice is based reflect a subjective view that the need for substitute care is the product of personal difficulties. We argue that it is this view which is a primary origin of class bias in foster care. Consider this view put forth by Charles Loring Brace in 1880:

The very constitution, too, of an agricultural and democratic community favors the probability of a poor child's succeeding. When placed in a farmer's family, he grows up as one of their number, and shares in all the social influences of the class. The peculiar temptations to which he has been subject—such, for instance, as stealing and vagrancy—are reduced to a minimum; his self-respect is raised, and the chances of success held out to a laborer in this country, with the influence of school and religion soon raise him far above the class from which he sprang.[14]

Reviewing recent foster care literature suggests that while the vocabulary has changed, the assumptions about problems that generate the need for substitute care, the goals held out for those in need, and the essential services to be rendered by the foster care system have remained similar to those identified by Brace and his contemporaries. Although substitute care for middle-class children is regarded as a service for the convenience of the family rather than as an occasion for the reform of the child and its parents, child welfare services take on a different cast. In this view foster care implies the need for some form of "casework or other *treatment* service" during the course of which public or charitable funds will be expended. Because the population served by the foster care professional is identified as having "problems," those who fall into the category are marked by social stigma.

Two interpretations account for why foster care users are labeled problematic. First, they depart from the middle-class norm of the unified nuclear family. Secondly, this departure from the norm is in turn associated with an inability to acquire an adequate income. The need for financial assistance in arranging substitute child care is not viewed neutrally, but is taken as evidence of a problematic population. Piore observes a similar process in his analysis of the role of professional discretion in the administration of public assistance:

The dependency view generalized the client's inability to maintain a stable family relationship or hold down a full-time job which made them eligible for assistance, to a more fundamental inability to cope effectively with the social and economic environment in which they found themselves. This view thus placed the Department *in loco parentis* to the client and her children.[15]

These observations apply to the foster care field as well. Many members of the social work profession have concluded that ". . . social disorganization or personality disorders of parents [of children in foster care] are so severe as to affect their ability to provide adequate parental care, . . ."[16] and that the need for foster care is prompted by some form of "parental inability."[17] As professionally defined then, substitute care is not an arrangement of choice, available to anyone, but it is a service available for a particular group of people (mostly lower class) who, by definition, are incapable of providing for the well-being of their children.

The apparent contradiction between benevolent intent toward, and antagonistic evaluation of, families in foster care further contributes to stigmatization in the system. Consider, for example, yet another opposition of contradictory principles:

The principal weakness of the boarding-out system, lies in the fact that it is founded on two opposite principles. The first is, confidence in the benevolence and honesty of human nature. The second, distrust of its selfishness and dishonesty. The former is expressed in the affectionate title of foster-parent and the latter in the elaborate supervision by which his conduct is watched and reported on to the Guardians. I am aware that all human transactions are governed by the principles of trust and distrust; but I confess that I do not know of any in which they are more strongly and more antagonistically appealed to than in the boarding out of pauper children.[18]

Once the system is limited to the poor (or black) their stigma in turn defines the system. Moreover, the *reasons* for placement of children of lower-income families add further to the process of stigmatization, because they are concentrated on parental problems. Commenting on findings that indicate this, Shyne says:

The proportion of non-white children was higher in the parent behavior, parent incapacity, and socio-economic stress groups. There is no reason to assume that other problems—out-of-wedlock pregnancy and birth, child behavior and handicap, and psychosocial stress—are less common among non-whites. Rather, one would assume that underrepresentation of non-whites in these problem groups reflects, in part at least, the lesser availability of service.[19]

The official foster care system then is populated mostly by the poor, those who for various reasons cannot seek help elsewhere. However, once these children enter the system they become trapped in it. Martin Wolins summarizes the foster care cycle:

Having defined foster care as an either/or situation, the "either" consisting of the child being left with his family, the parents continue with little outside attention until a relatively high threshold of community awareness or tolerance is surmounted. At this time, we remove the child and are saddened to report that the families themselves were severely deteriorated at the time of placement and their accessibility to treatment was questionable. Once the children are in care, parent-child contact and parent-agency contact decreases and, in many cases, ceases to exist. The children grow older, and begin to manifest an increase in emotional problems.

Children of hard-to-reach parents become hard to place. They grow into adulthood in foster care and the parents are less available to them and to treatment.[20]

Foster care is an example of a "treatment" system set up to aid the poor and the deviant, which also ensures that the society's worst suspicions about them become true and remain so. How the foster care system generates this self-fulfilling prophesy is the subject we next consider.

FOSTER CARE AS A CLASS-BOUND SYSTEM: THE CONSEQUENCES

To explore further the theme of class bias, we trace each stage of the process, starting first with the set of circumstances that propels families into foster care, then considering the duration in care, what happens while children are in care, and concluding with a review of the relationship of foster parents and professionals. In each instance a central topic will be the consequences of the class-bound nature of the foster care system.

How Do People Get Into the System?

The foster care system can be characterized as suffering from confusion of agency resources with the services that clients need or want. Professionals' responses to requests for service are likely to be confined by their bias in perceiving problems and their preferences for particular solutions. By narrowly construing the conditions precipitating the need for substitute care and by providing few alternatives, the foster care system contributes to the removal of children from the nuclear family. Because the system provides only a limited range of relatively drastic and stigmatizing options, people generally avoid using it. In fact, foster care is used only by those who have no other choice. As noted in the first section, only about one-fifth of all children in some form of substitute care are in the foster care system.

Though a variety of conditions precipitate the need for care (including physical incapacity of the parents, family problems, out-of-wedlock birth, neglect and abuse, emotional problems of child or parent, and socioeconomic stress), few if any of these are restricted to one class. For example, recent studies of child abuse show a perceptible number occurring among the nonpoor.[21]

Tables 2–3 and 2–4 give a picture of the distribution by class of conditions that lead to foster family care. In only two categories is the proportion of Class I, II, and III significantly larger than this group's proportion of the total sample. These categories, out-of-wedlock infant and unwed mother, are a very specialized aspect of foster care, but represent two-thirds of all Class I, II, and III use of the system. On the other hand, the proportion of Class V was particularly high in categories such as "Parent Behavior" or "Socioeconomic Problem," for which middle-class families have alternative resources available. They can cope with such problems without reliance upon the child welfare system. In short, middle- and upper-class families do not choose to utilize the foster care system, while poor and low-income families use it because they are forced to. Because foster family care accounts for only one-fifth of all children in substitute care, we assume at the same time that low-income families also use other options to the extent possible.

A reasonable interpretation of the process, then, is that children get into foster care because nothing else is available.

TABLE 2–3

Socioeconomic Status of Family, by Reason for Request for Foster Placement, Percentage Distribution of Classes

Socioeconomic Status	Total	Out-of-Wedlock Infant	Unwed Mother	Parent Behavior	Parent Incapacity	Socio-economic Problem	Child Behavior	Psycho-social Problem	Child Incapacity
Class I, II, III	16 (123)	25 (59)	34 (19)	9 (13)	3 (2)	11 (6)	18 (14)	9 (8)	12 (2)
Class IV	32 (239)	43 (100)	34 (19)	15 (22)	37 (25)	23 (13)	32 (25)	34 (32)	19 (3)
Class V	52 (391)	32 (76)	32 (18)	77 (115)	60 (40)	67 (38)	51 (40)	57 (53)	69 (11)
Total Percent / *Total Number*	100 (753)	100 (235)	100 (56)	100 (150)	100 (67)	100 (57)	100 (79)	100 (93)	100 (16)

SOURCE: Tables 2–3 and 2–4 based on Ann W. Shyne, *The Need for Foster Care* (New York: Child Welfare League of America, 1969), recalculated to reflect the 753 cases in the eight problem groups in which socioeconomic status is known. Used by permission.

TABLE 2-4

Socioeconomic Status of Family, by Reason for Request for Foster Placement, Percentage Distribution of Reasons

Socioeconomic Status	Total	Out-of-Wedlock Infant	Unwed Mother	Parent Behavior	Parent Incapacity	Socio-economic Problem	Child Behavior	Psycho-social Problem	Child Incapacity
Class I, II, III	100 (123)	48 (59)	15 (19)	11 (13)	2 (2)	5 (6)	11 (14)	6 (8)	2 (2)
Class IV	100 (239)	42 (100)	8 (19)	9 (22)	10 (25)	5 (13)	10 (25)	13 (32)	1 (3)
Class V	100 (391)	19 (76)	5 (18)	29 (115)	10 (40)	10 (38)	10 (40)	14 (53)	3 (11)
Total Percent Total Number	100 (753)	31 (235)	7 (56)	20 (150)	9 (67)	8 (57)	10 (79)	12 (93)	2 (16)

SOURCE: Same as Table 2–3 on page 35 and used by permission.

The middle and upper classes seek correctives, for which they have resources, before placement becomes urgent. The poor and low-income classes, with few intermediate services available, must wait until exigencies become sufficiently serious to merit attention. By then professional preferences and the availability of resources (which in themselves evidence a circularity of reasoning) dominate the disposition of children in foster care. This grim conclusion is supported by experience and evidence. Richman describes "the tendency in child welfare to see clients' needs in terms of available services and facilities rather than as problems requiring solution." [22] Similarly, Briar found placement recommendations were directly related to the predominant placement policies of their employing agencies.[23] The dominance of worker preference is further corroborated by Shyne, who notes that "The caseworkers' judgments about the type of care appropriate for children differed considerably from the applicants' requests." [24]

Is Placement Temporary?

Foster care is presumably a temporary solution to a particular problem. Yet a fair number of children enter the foster care system, vanish from sight, and remain trapped in the system for long periods of time. Available data indicate that somewhere between one to three quarters of all the children in foster care are trapped there—the figures vary depending on how the estimates are made. For example, Jenkins' study indicates that about one-half of children who entered foster care in 1963 were discharged within three months.[25] But over half of those who stay for three months will stay on for two years or more. A subsequent review of data from the same study confirmed Jenkins' pessimistic analysis. "The major exodus out of care occurs during the first year after entry, when three out of 10 children leave," David Fanshel writes. "Thereafter is a rapid decline in the number of children discharged, so that at the end of 3½ years it has become only a modest outflow and most of the children then in care seem destined to spend their remaining years of childhood as foster children." [26] An earlier national study presents the bleakest picture of all. Joseph Reid writes in its conclusion:

There are 268,000 children in foster care in the United States; of these, 44,000 are in pre-adoptive homes, the remainder in [child care] institutions and foster family homes. In no more than 25 percent of the foster care cases in most of the nine communities studied was it probable that the child would return to his home.[27]

Followed up ten years later, 422 of the children—31 percent of the sample—had been in care ten or more years; only 24 percent left in less than three years.[28]

Poverty and living arrangements operate against early return to natural parents. For example, in the follow-up just noted, 55 percent of the families of long-term care children were "below subsistence standard." [29] Evidence on the relative length of placement of white, black, and Puerto Rican children is mixed or inconclusive.[30] The more likely explanation for differences of duration of stay in the foster care system is found in the initial reasons for placement. Physical illness of a mother is likely to lead to using foster care for only a short term, while family and children's problems are likely to lead to the longest placement duration.[31] Table 2–3 indicates that a higher proportion of poorer children enter foster care because of their parents' physical illness (parental incapacity), while higher income groups tend to use foster care to solve problems of longer duration, such as mental retardation or emotional illness.

One other perspective on duration should be noted. Maas

concludes that "the visibility of the child and his total situation is important if he is not to remain in long-term care." [32] He suggests that children and their parents become lost from the view of agencies charged with serving them. It is as if foster care will be temporary only if the child or parents are tenacious in being visible. This curiously reverses the roles of worker and client and is a telling comment on problems that seem inherent in foster family care.

So foster care seems to be temporary in situations that are essentially beyond the control of parent, child, or social caseworker—for example, the illness of a mother. In situations in the domain of social casework treatment (family problems, child's problems) on the other hand, temporary foster care is at the very least a misnomer. Duration is not particularly class linked, but is more a matter of the initial reason for placement, and differences in visibility.

What Happens to Children in Foster Care?

Questionnaire responses from county and state agencies providing foster care indicate that a majority regard the services they provide to children and parents as fair or poor. Voluntary agencies rated themselves somewhat better— depending on the specific item, 10 to 50 percent rated their services fair or poor. Both types of agencies rated their services to parents worse than those to children. [33]

It is not surprising that self-ratings appear to be so low. Only two-thirds of the placement decisions that are initially made are carried out (see Table 2–5). More serious, the desired placement seems least likely to be carried out for the poorest families. Comparing Tables 2–3 and 2–5, the three categories in which Classes I, II, and III were clustered were the categories in which the rate of ideal placement decisions

TABLE 2–5

Percentage of Ideal Placement Decisions Carried Out, by Type of Placement and by Reason for Request

Type of Placement	IDEAL		Out-of-Wedlock Infant	Unwed Mother	Parent Behavior	Parent Incapacity	Socio-economic Problem	Child Behavior	Child Psycho-social	Child Incapacity
	Total	Percent Carried Out								
Own home	416	59	—°	—°	66	49	41	74	70	—°
Adoptive home	326	66	70	—	47	—°	—°	—°	36	—°
Foster home	247	78	93	70	88	83	46	67	72	—
Normal institution	60	87	—°	—	—°	—°	—°	100	83	—
Special institution	77	68	—	—°	30	—°	—°	86	—°	75
Maternity home	55	89	—	89	—	—	—	—	—	—
Percent carried out		66	71	84	68	58	39	75	62	62
Total	1260 †		293	74	281	132	111	139	141	21

SOURCE: Ann W. Shyne, *The Need for Foster Care* (New York: Child Welfare League of America, 1969), p. 47. Used by permission.

° Fewer than 10 ideal decisions in the cell.

† Includes 79 "other" types of placement or "unable to estimate."

carried out was highest. Where there were fewer Class I, II, and III families fewer placement decisions were carried out.

A 1959 national study concludes that 40 to 50 percent of children in foster care show indications of maladjustment; and maladjustment increases with length of time in care.[34] Does the foster care system itself contribute to this phenomenon? While a clear answer is not possible, the number of foster placements is four or five for the average 13-year-old boy.[35] This suggests the background for what Maas calls the child's concept of his marginality.[36] The biological parents do not have custody of the child, and often do not have much contact with him. The foster parents are ever reminded of their temporary status. The child is somewhere in the middle. Presumably, the caseworker is to provide stability, but caseworker turnover is high and those who stay are often overburdened.

In fact, few agencies undertake studies to evaluate the adjustment of children during or after foster care. The studies that are done are essentially descriptive.[37] We know very little, for example, about the education that foster children receive, the state of their health, or what eventually happens to them. Children in foster care take their chances; poorer children take a greater chance.

Foster Parents and Professionals

The role of the foster parent is shaped by the child welfare profession. Professionals define the job, select those who fill it, place particular children with particular parents, and monitor and support the arrangement. They define the status and reward scheme for foster parents, from the level of payment to whether a foster child may visit his foster parents after he leaves their home. In the end, the role is anything but clear.

Historically, foster parents have been in an ambiguous situation. On the one hand, they are to be motivated by the desire to help a child in difficulty; on the other hand, they are paid. The state, not the children or parents, establishes the standards of performance. Beyond this, the foster parent role involves acting like a natural parent, a client, a staff member, a relative, and also includes some "unique" behavior.[38] Discussing the confusion that results, Wolins suggests: "One possible explanation is that the agency—initiator and authority in foster care arrangements—has not made the rules of the game clear to the other players. It may be that the agency is itself not sure about the rules." [39] It does appear, however, that the "rules" result in foster parents with few rights but many responsibilities.

Scanty data indicate that foster parents come predominantly from the upper-lower and lower-middle classes. For example:

The typical subject was a woman about 40 years old who had been married a decade or more and was apt to have had at least one child of her own. She had had two or more years of high school and came from a rather modest, almost rural background. She tended to be home-centered, having discontinued employment after marriage. She had been a foster parent for five years or more and had cared for an average of five to ten children. She tended to be enthusiastic about foster parenthood, seeing this as a very meaningful kind of activity.[40]

Foster fathers tend to be blue-collar workers. Their income, slightly higher than the U.S. median, reflects the large numbers who are craftsmen or foremen (see Tables 2–6, 2–7, and 2–8).

We expect that agencies seldom attempt middle-class recruitment, and can only speculate on the reasons for this bias. Perhaps middle-class families without children prefer adopting them, while most families with children already reside in

T A B L E   2 – 6

Percentage Distribution of Foster Fathers by Their Earnings at Time of Study and Five Years Earlier, with Comparative Percentage Distribution of Families in the United States

| Earnings | FOSTER FATHERS (N = 81) | | U.S. Families (1958) |
	At Time of Study	Five Years Earlier	
Under $2000	1%	1%	14%
$2001–$3000	2	14	10
$3001–$4000	10	21	11
$4001–$5000	17	35	13
$5001–$6000	30	14	14
$6001–$7000	19	6	11
$7001–$8000	12	4	8
More than $8000	4	4	19
Unemployed, retired, etc.	5	1	—
Total	100	100	100
Median Income	$5,563	$4,379	$5,087

SOURCE: David Fanshel, *Foster Parenthood: A Role Analysis* (Minneapolis: University of Minnesota Press, 1966), p. 57. Copyright 1966 by the University of Minnesota. Used by permission of the publisher and D. Fanshel.

T A B L E   2 – 7

Percentage Distribution of Foster Fathers by Their Education (N = 81)

Amount of Education	Foster Fathers
Never attended school	0%
Some grade school	21
Completed grade school	19
Some high school	15
Completed high school	22
Some college	7
Completed college	5
Other (trade school, etc.)	10
Unknown, no response	1
Total	100

SOURCE: David Fanshel, *Foster Parenthood: A Role Analysis* (Minneapolis: University of Minnesota Press, 1966), p. 56. Copyright 1966 by the University of Minnesota. Used by permission of the publisher and D. Fanshel.

TABLE 2-8

Foster Father Occupation (U.S. Census Classification; N = 973)

	Percent
Professional, technician, manager, official, proprietor, farm owner, farm manager	15
Clerical, sales, service, etc.	20
Craftsmen, foremen, factory operative	58
Laborer, farm laborer	7
Total	100

SOURCE: Martin Wolins, *Selecting Foster Parents* (New York: Columbia University Press, 1963), p. 201, Table 25. Used by permission of the publisher and Martin Wolins.

the suburbs and do not have sufficient room to house an additional child. So the foster family care system consists of middle-class workers, with upper-lower-class and lower-middle-class foster parents serving as intermediaries to predominantly lower-class clients.

What does the foster care system invest in its parents and what does that reveal about class bias? Very little in training, remuneration, or status. A recent survey found that agencies rely on traditional supervisory and orientation sessions to provide most of the training.[41] Little or no training in child care is offered. Little is done to involve foster parents in the broader concerns of child welfare and the broader implications of the family situations in which they are implicated. As Fanshel notes:

This paternalism shows in a most obnoxious form in settings in which the myth exists that foster parents are clients. Even in agencies where the notion of clienthood is rejected, there remains the illusion that foster parents can be "treated" by casework techniques to transform them from what they basically are into agents of social workers.[42]

The lack of training can have implications for the quality of care, particularly if the child involved is disturbed. In this regard Fanshel argues that agencies have "exploited foster parents by placing children in their homes when it has been known in advance that the foster parents lacked the capacity to deal with the behavior the child and his family would show." [43]

As for payment, a survey found that only one out of four agencies felt their lowest rate for care covered the actual cost of a child's care.[44] Only one in four agencies paid parents a fee for service.[45] In short, foster parents are in an unenviable financial position: they come from lower socioeconomic strata and provide the majority of foster homes and receive "almost unbelievably low basic payment . . . in relation to the costs of providing care." [46]

Most agencies think they should work toward having professional foster parents "who are experienced in child care, have a commitment to the job, receive training and supervision from the agency, and receive a salary." [47] Yet only one-fourth of the agencies felt they had parents who qualify under this definition. Further, the results of the question about salaries for foster parents show a very "conservative" view.[48] And the chance of a change in the situation of foster parents seems remote. Professionals have been careful to draw and maintain a clear line between themselves and foster parents. The professionals' approach seeks to define the children as having problems, and the foster parents as requiring supervision. This affirms a continuing role for the professional, but reinforces the "treatment" approach to substitute care. The class and racial composition of foster children and foster parents provides further legitimization of these approaches. Class roles are maintained up and down the line; it can hardly be an accident.

The quality of foster care services, as this section indicates, is open to serious question. Many children are placed when preventive services might have alleviated that necessity; many are trapped in long-term care and lead the uncertain and stigmatized lives of foster children. The system is so structured that professionals are not accountable for children in their care, and foster parents (who are accountable) have insufficient resources to provide adequate care. In the light of this, what might be done?

WHAT SHOULD BE DONE?

Criticism of the quality of foster family care is not particularly new. For example, the Citizens' Committee for Children of New York has documented the 25-year child welfare crisis in New York City and the lack of response to it.[49] Two recent reports provide an idea of the professional view of problems and appropriate responses. One reports on a national survey of attitudes and practices in foster care.[50] Another reports the findings of the Ad Hoc Committee on Foster Care of Children of the New York State Board of Social Welfare.[51]

Stone notes that "the strongest wind blowing is the urgency of the need for change in the present system of foster care and the recognition of it by those in practice." [52] The data suggest that biological parents are receiving poor quality service, that aftercare services are limited, that agencies have doubts about the quality of services to children in care, that the turnover rate among personnel is high, that little is known about what is being accomplished by the foster care system, and that comprehensive community and agency planning are needed. Three insights are offered. First, Stone says that "the energies of [agencies] are spent largely in keeping up with the demand for services, with little time and thought given to innovations or the development of better methods. *Few changes in techniques or methods of providing foster care were reported."* [53] Second, recruitment techniques for foster parents are not successful, monthly payments to them are extremely low and may not even cover their costs, and little training is offered to them.

Third, the changes that agencies recommend reflect continuing confidence in the effectiveness of improving *professional* conditions. "Lack of staff and lack of staff training were mentioned most often as weaknesses of their programs. Thus, staffing is seen as the crucial pivot on which good foster care services rest." [54] But professionalization and innovation may be incompatible. All available studies support the conclusion that not many innovations are taking place in the use of personnel.[55] In brief, Stone's report suggests:

1. Little new is going on in the field of foster care despite a widespread feeling that what is going on is pretty much unacceptable.
2. What change is occurring is worker oriented.
3. Foster parents, despite spending more time with the children than any other component of the system, receive the least attention.

The 1971 report of the Ad Hoc Committee on Foster Care of Children presented a 14 point resolution that embodied the substance of its year long study of foster care in New York City. In general the recommendations of the committee are unexceptionable, with proposals to expand personnel, coordinate services, improve planning, and increase efficiency. Implementation of the recommendations would produce "immeasurable social benefits" and save "millions of dollars," the Ad Hoc Committee said. Most striking in the committee report, as in the Stone report are recommendations for expansion in precisely those areas where the profession has indicated that current practice is unacceptable. Recommendations seem to suggest more and better of *what is accepted as unacceptable!*

We do not propose specific recommendations, but offer instead a redefinition of the issue. Central to a system of substitute care that will work for those who might have need of it is a change in the terms of reference. Crucial to this needed redefinition are a broader notion of the universe involved in substitute care and a different understanding of the nature of substitute care options to be made available.

The circumstances of children in foster care cannot be understood in isolation from all children in substitute care. To do so leads to a grim conclusion. The modern foster care system appears almost to have been deliberately designed to assign a lower level of resources to the poor who are trapped in its care. It seems as if the function of foster care is to contain poor children in a low-quality system of care without facing the similarity of poor children to children in other substitute care systems who get different magnitudes and quality of resources, without facing the differentials in the standards of care, and without facing the effects of these differentials on the future life chances of children.

How this dual system of care came about is an unfolding of 200 years of history, which can be traced back to policies of child indenture, placement in almshouses and then in substitute community care. Child welfare is still trapped in the history of the breakup of the poor law. Its mission remains the welfare of poor children and not the needs of all children. The strategy of humane and professional reform seeks to improve the quality of provision of care to those who are poor. Not surprisingly, reform is constantly frustrated in its search for more resources, without an appreciation of the broader forces that limit its scope for redistribution.

Professionalism is of course a way of enhancing the quality

of care as measured not by the level of resources available to children or their foster parents, but by the number of professionals who work with parents and children and by the level of their educational achievement.[56] But professionalization simply reinforces the foster care dilemma. In the end, professionals can do only what they know—treat. By taking a treatment approach they reinforce the societal view that there are two separate groups of children. The damage done by the poor care available to foster children operates in turn to confirm this prediction. Professionals and the adjustment difficulties foster care children experience, and the poor system of provision they are both enclosed in, complement each other. The system makes the children and their families sick. The sick children and families confirm the professional prediction of maladjustment. This reinforces the conviction that what is required is what professionals are trained to supply—treatment. The more limited the effectiveness of the treatment approach, the more determined is the effort to augment the numbers of professionals and the quality of training they acquire. This is the thrust of the reports cited earlier. This is why their recommendations will compound rather than resolve the problems.

Intractable problems can best be resolved by defining them. This chapter is an attempt to sketch out the direction that such a redefinition might take. We need first to recognize the class bias of the existing foster care system, and instead to view all children needing and receiving substitute care as a group. Research on the operation of this dual system of care needs to be undertaken, with its inequities and inequalities documented. Within this broader perspective, alternative solutions—in service options, in delivery systems, in system administration, in personnel—will become clear. Such reforms will accept as their terms of reference an approach that is non-treatment oriented. To be more specific, it will provide treatment where it is required, but not as a consequence of the condition of poverty. Reform should eliminate the class bias of the present foster care system and should create a single system of substitute parental care that would be available to all children. Providing a full range of substitute care options (including related preventive measures) will permit a closer match of condition to preferred solution. It will also permit professionals to move away from their tendency to confuse conditions that occasion a request for substitute care with the particular sort of service they manage.

NOTES

1. Helen D. Stone, *Reflections on Foster Care: A Report of a National Survey of Attitudes and Practices* (New York: Child Welfare League of America, 1969), p. 28.
2. 1970 Census, Population Characteristics, no. 212, February 1, 1971, Series P–20, Table 4.
3. Stone, *Reflections on Foster Care*, p. 9.
4. Stone, *Reflections on Foster Care*, p. 25.
5. 1970 Census, Population Characteristics, no. 212.
6. 1970 Census, Population Characteristics, no. 212.
7. Richard R. Rowe *et al.*, *Child Care in Massachusetts: The Public Responsibility*, a study for the Massachusetts Advisory Council on Education (Cambridge, Mass.: February 1972), p. 28, Table 3–2.
8. Shirley Jenkins and Elaine Rubenstein, "Families of Children in Foster Care" (paper presented to the National Conference on Social Welfare, San Francisco, Calif., May 28, 1968), p. 4.
9. Ann W. Shyne, *The Need for Foster Care, An Incidence Study of Requests for Foster Care and Agency Response in Seven Metropolitan Areas* (New York: Child Welfare League of America, 1969).
10. Shirley Jenkins and Mignon Sauber, *Paths to Child Placement: Family Situations Prior to Foster Care* (New York: Community Council of Greater New York, 1966), p. 180.
11. Jenkins and Sauber, *Paths to Child Placement*, p. 180.

12. Jenkins and Sauber, *Paths to Child Placement,* p. 122.
13. Shyne, *The Need for Foster Care.*
14. Charles Loring Brace, "What Is the Best Method for the Care of Poor and Vicious Children," *Journal of Social Science,* 2 (1880), 93–98 as quoted by Robert H. Bremner, ed., *Children and Youth in America: A Documentary History,* vol. II (Cambridge, Mass.: Harvard University Press, 1971).
15. Michael J. Piore, "Racial Negotiations: The Massachusetts Welfare Confrontation," mimeographed, February 1970.
16. *Standards for Foster Family Care Services* (New York: Child Welfare League of America, 1959), p. 2.
17. *Standards for Foster Family Care Services,* p. 7.
18. Written by a Mr. Bowyer in 1874 and quoted in Sir William Chance, *Children Under the Poor Law* (London: Swan, Sonnenschein and Co., 1897), p. 225.
19. Shyne, *The Need for Foster Care,* p. 71.
20. Martin Wolins and Mary Jane Owen, "Foster Care: Assumptions, Evidence, and Alternatives: An Exploratory Analysis," prepared for the Joint Commission on the Mental Health of Children, mimeographed, n.d., p. 4. They are using here the evidence of Bernice Boehm, *Deterrents to the Adoption of Children in Foster Care* (New York: Child Welfare League of America, 1958).
21. Children's Hospital Medical Center, "Study of Social Illness in Children," mimeographed (Boston, November 1971), p. 6, and David G. Gil, *Violence Against Children: Physical Child Abuse in the United States* (Cambridge, Harvard University Press, 1970).
22. Leon H. Richman, "Differential Planning in Child Welfare," *Child Welfare,* 37, no. 7 (July 1958), 5.
23. Scott Briar, "Clinical Judgment in Foster Care Placement," *Child Welfare,* 42, no. 4 (April 1963), 161–168.
24. Shyne, *The Need for Foster Care,* p. 72.
25. Shirley Jenkins, "Duration of Foster Care—Some Relevant Antecedent Variables," *Child Welfare,* 46, no. 8 (October 1967), 450–456.
26. David Fanshel, "The Exit of Children from Foster Care," *Child Welfare,* 50, no. 2 (February 1971), 80.
27. Henry S. Maas, and Richard E. Engler, Jr., *Children in Need of Parents* (New York: Columbia University Press, 1959), p. 379.
28. Henry S. Maas, "Children in Long-Term Foster Care," *Child Welfare,* 48, no. 6 (June 1969), 323.
29. Maas, "Children in Long-Term Foster Care," p. 328.

30. Fanshel, "The Exit of Children from Foster Care," pp. 70, 71.
31. Jenkins, "Duration of Foster Care."
32. Maas, "Children in Long-Term Foster Care," p. 332.
33. Stone, *Reflections on Foster Care*, p. 23, Tables X, XI.
34. Henry S. Maas, "Highlights of the Foster Care Project: Introduction," *Child Welfare*, 38, no. 7 (July 1959).
35. W. J. Ambinder, "The Extent of Successive Placements Among Boys in Foster Family Homes," *Child Welfare*, 44, no. 7 (July 1965).
36. Maas, "Children in Long-Term Foster Care," p. 333.
37. See Stone, *Reflections on Foster Care*, p. 25.
38. Martin Wolins, *Selecting Foster Parents* (New York: Columbia University Press, 1963), p. 17.
39. Wolins, *Selecting Foster Parents*.
40. David Fanshel, *Foster Parenthood: A Role Analysis* (Minneapolis: University of Minnesota Press, 1966), p. 44.
41. Stone, *Reflections on Foster Care*, p. 25.
42. David Fanshel, *Foster Care in Question* (New York: Child Welfare League of America, 1967), p. 229.
43. Fanshel, *Foster Care in Question*, p. 229.
44. Stone, *Reflections on Foster Care*, p. 33.
45. Stone, *Reflections on Foster Care*, p. 31, Table XV.
46. Stone, *Reflections on Foster Care*, p. 33.
47. Stone, *Reflections on Foster Care*, p. 31.
48. Stone, *Reflections on Foster Care*, Table XV.
49. Citizens' Committee for Children, *A Dream Deferred* (New York: Citizens' Committee for Children, 1971).
50. Stone, *Reflections on Foster Care*.
51. *A Program of Action for Children in Need*, Ad Hoc Committee on Foster Care of Children, New York State Board of Social Welfare, 1971.
52. Stone, *Reflections on Foster Care*, p. 40.
53. Stone, *Reflections on Foster Care*, p. 39, italics added.
54. Stone, *Reflections on Foster Care*, p. 27.
55. Stone, *Reflections on Foster Care*, p. 28.
56. For example, the rate of full-time professional child welfare employees of state and local public welfare agencies increased by 67 percent between 1955 and 1969 (from 0.9 to 1.5 per 10,000 children). Yet the extent and growth of professionalization has contributed little to abating the persistent crisis in foster care.

3

Institutions for Children

DAVID G. GIL

The purpose of this chapter is to examine institutional care for dependent and neglected children in the United States and social policies implicit in this care. From my point of view,[1] such social policies are not always fully comprehended even by the people involved in implementing them. Therefore, we will be exploring such possibly unexpected questions as the social issues dealt with by this type of child care, its social functions, purposes, and value premises, and its multi-faceted consequences.

THE SCOPE OF INSTITUTIONAL CARE FOR CHILDREN

According to the 1970 White House Conference on Children,[2] about 74,000 children were living in child welfare institutions for neglected, dependent, and emotionally disturbed children in 1969. This constitutes a rate of 1 per thousand children under age 18. One generation earlier, in 1933, 144,000 children, or 3.4 per thousand children, lived in such institutions. Although institutional care for children has clearly decreased, the rate of decline appears to have slowed in recent years.

The change appears to be primarily the result of a shift in child welfare philosophy toward foster family care rather than of a decrease in the number of children cared for away from their own homes and families. The number of these children in placement increased between 1933 and 1969 from 249,000 to 323,000 children. As the number of children in the population increased, the rate per thousand of children in placement decreased only moderately during this period— from 5.9 to 4.5. In 1933, children's institutions accounted for 58 percent of children in child welfare placements; in 1969 institutional care accounted for 23 percent of such placements. Comparative figures are provided in Table 3–1.

It needs to be noted, however, that neglected, dependent, and emotionally disturbed children now constitute less than 25 percent of all children in institutional care. In 1960, nearly 62,000 children lived in various types of "correctional institutions" (training schools, jails, diagnostic and reception centers, and so on); over 78,000 lived in institutions for mentally handicapped, in mental hospitals, and in residential treat-

TABLE 3–1

Children under Age 18 in Foster Family Care and in Child Welfare Institutions for Neglected, Dependent, and Emotionally Disturbed Children (Numbers and Rates per 1,000 Children)

Year	TOTAL		FOSTER FAMILY CARE		INSTITUTIONAL CARE	
	Number	Rate	Number	Rate	Number	Rate
1933	249,000	5.9	105,000	2.5	144,000	3.4
1969	323,000	4.5	249,000	3.4	74,000	1.0

SOURCE: *Profiles of Children*, 1970 White House Conference on Children (Washington, D.C.: Government Printing Office, 1970), p. 147, Table 107.

ment centers; and nearly 25,000 lived in institutions for physically disabled children.[3] While the number of neglected, dependent, and emotionally disturbed children in institutions has been declining steadily, the number in correctional institutions and in institutions for mentally disabled children has been increasing significantly.[4]

We have not, as yet, revealed the entire scope of institutional care for children in the United States. Children residing in private boarding schools ought to be included in the total number of children in institutional care. It seems significant in this context that the Census Bureau does not count private boarding schools as institutions. This point will be commented on below. Systematic data are not available on the numbers and characteristics of children in private boarding schools. Incomplete statistics of the U.S. Office of Education suggest, however, that about 150,000 children resided in private elementary and secondary boarding schools in 1961.[5]

The scope of institutional care for children in the United States can now be summarized. On any day in 1960 about 400,000 children under age 18 resided in some type of institutional setting. About 20 percent were in institutions for neglected, dependent, and disturbed children, about 15 percent in correctional institutions, about 20 percent in institutions for the mentally disabled, about 6 percent in institutions for the physically disabled, and about 38 percent in private boarding schools.

The 1970 census of the institutional population is not available, as this is written. Assuming that the population of child care institutions has increased at about the same rate as the total population of children,[6] it may be estimated that on any day in 1970 about 432,000 children were in institutional care. That is, there were 70,000 children in correctional institutions, 100,000 children in institutions for the mentally disabled, 27,000 in institutions for physically disabled children,

162,000 in private boarding schools, and 73,000 in institutions for neglected, dependent and disturbed children. An overall rate of institutional care, including child welfare, correctional, and private institutions, works out to about 6.2 per thousand children. Chances are, the 1970 census will show that correctional institutions and institutions for mentally disabled took slightly larger proportions of children, institutions for the physically disabled and private boarding schools took about the same proportion, and institutions for neglected, dependent, and disturbed children took a somewhat smaller proportion of institutionalized children.

Several questions are suggested by the foregoing review of trends in institutional care for children. What is the meaning of, or how "real" is, the decline in the number of neglected, dependent, and disturbed children in child welfare institutions while their numbers increase in other types of institutions? Are children labeled "neglected and dependent" and children in correctional institutions different? Is institutional care bad for the first, but good for the second? How do children in private boarding schools differ from those in institutions for neglected and dependent children? Why is private institutional care still considered suitable when child welfare institutions are increasingly viewed as inappropriate? Why are private boarding schools never mentioned in the professional literature of child welfare?

Some quantitative information about children's institutions themselves seems now in order. The best existing source is a census of children's residential institutions conducted in 1966.[7] Tables 3–2, 3–3, and 3–4 summarize some findings of this census.[8] In short, there were 3,763 residential institutions for children in the United States, about half under charitable auspices, a third public, and the remainder operated for private profit. Institutions for dependent and neglected children were largely under voluntary, nonprofit auspices. Public insti-

T A B L E   3–2

Types and Auspices of Children's Residential Institutions in the United States—September 1965

Type of Institution	AUSPICES AND NUMBER OF INSTITUTIONS [°]			
	Public	Volun-tary	Propri-etary	Total [†]
Maternity homes for unmarried girls				
Separate facilities	2	170	1	174
Facilities joint with infant or child care [‡]	—	38	—	38
Institutions for dependent and neglected children				
Nurseries joint with maternity homes [‡]	—	36	—	36
Temporary shelters	45	37	—	82
Institutions for dependent and neglected	244	1,090	63	1,397
Institutions for delinquent and predelinquent children				
Detention facilities	242	5	—	247
Institutions for delinquents and predelinquents	276	103	21	400
Institutions for emotionally disturbed children				
Residential treatment centers	5	141	18	166
Psychiatric inpatient facilities	119	17	12	149
Institutions for handicapped children				
Facilities for mentally retarded	152	128	416	701
Facilities for physically handicapped	136	202	31	373
Total institutions	1,221	1,967	562	3,763

SOURCE: Shirley A. Star and Alma M. Kuby, *Number and Kinds of Children's Residential Institutions in the United States,* U.S. Department of Health, Education, and Welfare, Children's Bureau (Washington, D.C.: Government Printing Office, 1967), Table 2.

° Includes Puerto Rico and the Virgin Islands.

† Includes 13 institutions of private, but otherwise unknown, auspices not shown in preceding detail columns.

‡ Figures for these two categories would be identical except for the fact that two of the maternity homes are joint with facilities for mentally retarded children.

TABLE 3-3

Types and Auspices of Public Children's Residential Institutions in the United States—September 1965

Type of Institution	AUSPICES AND NUMBER OF PUBLIC INSTITUTIONS °				
	Federal	State	County	Muni-cipal	Total Public †
Maternity homes for unmarried girls					
Separate facilities	—	2	—	—	2
Facilities joint with infant or child care	—	—	—	—	—
Institutions for dependent and neglected children					
Nurseries joint with maternity homes	—	—	—	—	—
Temporary shelters	2	4	34	5	45
Institutions for dependent and neglected	98	28	108	10	244
Institutions for delinquent and predelinquent children					
Detention facilities	—	8	226	8	242
Institutions for delinquents and predelinquents	2	211	56	7	276
Institutions for emotionally dis-turbed children					
Residential treatment centers	—	3	2	—	5
Psychiatric inpatient facilities	1	114	1	3	119
Institutions for handicapped children					
Facilities for mentally retarded	—	149	1	2	152
Facilities for physically handicapped	4	122	3	6	136
Total public institutions	107	641	431	41	1,221

SOURCE: Shirley A. Star and Alma M. Kuby, *Number and Kinds of Children's Residential Institutions in the United States,* U.S. Department of Health, Education, and Welfare, Children's Bureau (Washington, D.C.: Government Printing Office, 1967), Table 3.
° Includes Puerto Rico and the Virgin Islands.
† Includes one institution of public, but otherwise unknown, auspices not shown in preceding detail columns.

TABLE 3–4

Types and Auspices of Voluntary Children's Residential Institutions in the
United States—September 1965

	AUSPICES AND NUMBER OF VOLUNTARY INSTITUTIONS °					
Type of Institution	Protes- tant	Cath- olic	Jewish	Secular	Unspec- ified	Total Voluntary
Maternity homes for unmarried girls						
Separate facilities	56	43	2	64	5	170
Facilities joint with infant or child care †	4	20	—	12	2	38
Institutions for dependent and neglected children						
Nurseries joint with maternity homes †	4	18	—	12	2	36
Temporary shelters	10	6	2	15	4	37
Institutions for dependent and neglected	397	273	24	337	59	1,090
Institutions for delinquent and predelinquent children						
Detention facilities	—	—	—	5	—	5
Institutions for delinquents and predelinquents	15	61	1	22	4	103
Institutions for emotionally disturbed children						
Residential treatment centers	34	24	11	62	10	141
Psychiatric inpatient facilities	—	3	3	11	—	17
Institutions for handicapped children						
Facilities for mentally retarded	16	36	2	68	6	128
Facilities for physically handicapped	9	19	3	162	9	202
Total institutions	545	503	48	770	101	1,967

Source: Shirley A. Star and Alma M. Kuby, *Number and Kinds of Children's Residential Institutions in the United States,* U.S. Department of Health, Education, and Welfare, Children's Bureau (Washington, D.C.: Government Printing Office, 1967), Table 4.

° Includes Puerto Rico and Virgin Islands.

† Figures for these two categories would be identical except for the fact that two of the maternity homes are joint with facilities for mentally retarded children.

tutions accounted for the largest number of facilities for delinquent children, as might be expected. Proprietary institutions were largely devoted to mentally retarded children. The federal government has little role in children's institutions of any sort; states and counties support most of them. The large majority of voluntary, nonprofit institutions are under religious auspices.

The authors of this census surveyed over 2,300 of these institutions. Although they secured an extensive range of information, no data were secured on the ethnic or socioeconomic background of the children, the goals or finances of the institutions, or the outcome of placement. Such information is essential; its omission seems significant.

SELECTION OF CHILDREN BY INCOME AND SOCIAL STATUS

The scarcity of systematic social information concerning the children in residential care seems strange in a society as data-hungry as ours. We know that boarding schools of the U.S. Bureau of Indian Affairs held about 5,000 children in 1960 and that private boarding schools cater, by and large, to families who can pay substantial amounts. Beyond that we have no aggregate data on the total population of these boarding schools.

As for institutions serving dependent, neglected, and delinquent children, we can only infer that the families of children in these institutions are poor or in marginal economic circumstances. This may be deduced from a 1966 study of the financing of public services prepared for the Joint Economic Committee of Congress. Contributions of families to the cost of care in such institutions ranged from less than 4 percent in institutions serving delinquents to about 6.5 percent in institutions for dependent children.[9] These so-called "user charges" may be taken as a rough measure of the economic capacity of the families of these children.

In view of the marginal family income of children in child welfare institutions, it is not surprising that nonwhites are overrepresented. According to a 1960 study:

. . . the rate of institutionalization of nonwhite children in these types of institutions was 6.3 per 1,000, which was 58 percent above the rate of 4.0 white children per 1,000. Although nonwhite children then comprised 13 percent of the nation's children they comprised 20 percent of children residing in child welfare institutions. The great majority of the nonwhite children in institutions were Negro (89 percent), but 8 percent were American Indian and 3 percent were of other races.[10]

Tables 3–5 and 3–6 show the racial distribution for different types of institutions, the rate of institutionalization by age, and a comparison of these data for 1950 and 1960. It is

TABLE 3–5

Rate of Institutionalization of Children, by Race and by Age, 1960 and 1950 (Rates per 1,000 Children)

	1960		1950	
Age	White	Nonwhite	White	Nonwhite
Under 5	0.7	0.9	1.1	0.8
5–9	2.4	2.0	3.8	1.8
10–14	5.1	7.4	7.3	5.5
15–19	8.9	19.0	8.6	14.1
20	8.6	21.7	7.8	17.6
Total	4.0	6.3	4.8	5.3

SOURCE: Seth Low, *America's Children and Youth Institutions, 1950–1960–1964*, U.S. Department of Health, Education, and Welfare, Children's Bureau (Washington, D.C.: Government Printing Office, 1965), Table 2.

TABLE 3-6
Number of Children under 20 Years of Age in Institutions, by Race and by Type of Institution, 1960 and 1950 °

Type of Institution	1960					1950				
	NUMBER OF CHILDREN			PERCENT DISTRIBUTION		NUMBER OF CHILDREN			PERCENT DISTRIBUTION	
	Total	White	Nonwhite	White	Nonwhite	Total	White	Nonwhite	White	Nonwhite
All institutions	282,571	229,289	53,282	81.1	18.9	240,782	210,464	30,318	87.4	12.6
Welfare	75,060	66,538	8,522	88.6	11.4	101,239	95,491	5,748	94.3	5.7
Homes for dependent and neglected children	70,164	62,307	7,857	88.8	11.2	95,073	89,771	5,302	94.4	5.6
Homes for unwed mothers	2,631	2,227	404	84.6	15.4	2,291	2,101	190	91.7	8.3
Homes for the aged and dependent	2,265	2,004	261	88.5	11.5	3,875	3,619	256	93.4	6.6
Correctional	87,323	58,593	28,730	67.1	32.9	56,664	41,691	14,973	73.6	26.4
Training schools for juvenile delinquents	43,793	29,940	13,853	68.4	31.6	34,742	26,884	7,858	77.4	22.6
Prisons and reformatories	19,421	12,828	6,593	66.1	33.9	12,531	8,368	4,163	66.8	33.2
Local jails and workhouses	13,091	8,321	4,770	63.6	36.4	6,944	4,550	2,394	65.5	34.4
Detention homes	9,790	6,648	3,142	67.9	32.1	2,447	1,889	558	77.2	22.8

Diagnostic and reception centers	1,228	856	372	69.7	30.3	—†	—†	—†	—†	—†
Mental disabilities	92,821	81,542	11,279	87.8	12.2	57,288	51,945	5,343	90.7	9.3
Homes and schools for the mentally handicapped	73,664	65,768	7,896	89.3	10.7	46,265	43,230	3,035	93.4	6.6
Mental hospitals and residential treatment centers	19,157	15,774	3,383	82.3	17.7	11,023	8,715	2,308	79.1	20.9
Physical disabilities	27,367	22,616	4,751	82.6	17.4	25,591	21,337	4,254	83.4	16.6
Homes and schools for the physically handicapped	21,588	18,974	2,614	87.9	12.1	17,973	15,935	2,038	88.7	11.3
Tuberculosis hospitals	4,287	2,579	1,708	60.2	39.8	6,753	4,652	2,101	68.9	31.1
Chronic disease hospitals	1,492	1,063	429	71.2	28.8	865	750	115	86.7	13.3

SOURCE: Seth Low, *America's Children and Youth Institutions, 1950–1960–1964*, U.S. Department of Health, Education, and Welfare, Children's Bureau (Washington, D.C.: Government Printing Office, 1965).
° This table relates to children under 20 years of age (rather than under 21) in order to make possible a comparison of 1960 and 1950 data. Alaska and Hawaii are excluded.
† Not available.

noteworthy that, in Low's words, "the largest proportion of nonwhite children is found in the class of correctional institutions (33 percent)." [11] "More than half of all nonwhite children in institutions reside in correctional institutions (as compared with about one-fourth of the white)." [12]

The overrepresentation of nonwhites in child welfare institutions increased considerably between 1950 and 1960. Whereas the rate per thousand for white children decreased during the 1950s from 4.8 to 4.0, the rate for nonwhite children increased from 5.3 to 6.3. "In correctional institutions the number of nonwhite children rose 92 percent during the decade, more than double the increase in white children." [13] As for institutions for dependent and neglected children, the number of nonwhite children in these institutions increased during the 1950s by 48 percent, while the number of white children declined during this same period by 30.6 percent.[14]

Scanty as the foregoing aggregate information is, it seems clear enough: public and charitable institutions serve poor and minority children, whereas private boarding schools serve the affluent. We will discuss the meaning of those findings shortly. Many studies of local institutions, of the characteristics of children cared for in these institutions, and of placement practices, lend support to the foregoing conclusions. The following quote from Kadushin's comprehensive book [15] on child welfare services is illustrative:

. . . the Howard University School of Social Work conducted a study of the reasons for placement of a sample of 376 children at Junior Village, an institution for dependent and neglected children in Washington, D.C. As the report indicates: "Over half of the children were admitted because of the destitution of the person caring for them; 20 percent, because of the inadequacies of this person, usually a parent; about 15 percent, because of parental illness; and less than 4 percent, because of the child's behavior."

The general hypothesis of the study that placement of the children was the result of the "destitution of the parent rather than the result of unsatisfactory parental functioning"—was sustained. Nine of ten children in the sample were Negroes, and more than half were under six years of age when placed in the institution. A disconcerting tendency was that children placed in the institution because of family poverty were likely to remain there even longer than those placed because of parental inadequacy. Family poverty was defined "not as the simple absence of money, but a poverty compounded of poor education, poor health, poor housing, . . . unemployment and low wages." [16]

SOCIAL ISSUES DEALT WITH
BY RESIDENTIAL CHILDREN'S INSTITUTIONS

In every human society situations may occur when some children cannot, or should not, live with their parents. Residential children's institutions are one of several possible responses to such eventualities. Other responses are adoption, foster family care, indenture, slavery, abandonment, infanticide, and so on. These various responses may overlap. For instance, foster family care may include elements of indenture, and institutional care may include elements of abandonment or of slow infanticide.

The circumstances under which children will be separated from their parents may vary. Definitions of these circumstances will at times be quite precise, for example, "orphanhood," and at other times quite vague, for example, "emotional disturbance," "delinquency." Such factors as age, sex, social caste and class, economic circumstances, and minority status may affect the definitions. In present-day American society, for instance, a child of black, working-class parents will more likely be separated from his parents for truancy than will a child of white, professional parents.

Circumstances for separating children from parents are not always defined in terms of social, biological, or psychological deviance. Placement in residential institutions may be a normal procedure under specified circumstances in certain social groups. Thus, British and American aristocratic and upper-class families tend to transfer child-rearing responsibilities for their adolescent children to elite boarding schools, and many collective settlements in Israel tend to rear even their infants in residential children's institutions. Consequently, many successful members of the ruling elites in Great Britain, the United States, and Israel, have spent part or all of their childhood in child care institutions.

Since the beginning of colonization of the New World in the sixteenth century, residential care of children has been used for a variety of normal as well as deviant circumstances. Perhaps the first use of this method of socialization was boarding schools for American Indian children operated by Christian missionaries. In 1512 King Ferdinand of Spain promulgated a law according to which "all the sons of the caciques [Indian nobles appointed by the Spanish government] who are under 13 years of age are to be handed over to the friars of the Order of St. Francis so that the said friars teach them how to read and write and all things pertaining to Our Holy Catholic Faith; [the friars] are to keep these children for four years and then shall return them to their ecomenderos [Spanish colonists] so that they will teach other Indians." [17] About a century later, in 1609, Virginia Company officials authorized the "kidnapping" of Indian children in order to bring them up as Christians.[18] King Ferdinand's law and the Virginia Council's instructions to its resident governor reflect the arrogant, self-righteous, and cruel attitudes that underlie the practice, now in its fifth century, of placing American Indian children and youth in residential institutions, often against the wishes of their families and tribes, in

order to acculturate them to the values of the foreign con-
querors of their lands.

After the war of independence of the United States and a
long series of nearly genocidal wars of the young republic
against Indian tribes, child care institutions or boarding
schools were used with increasing frequency as important
tools of an oppressive colonial-type policy, referred to euphe-
mistically as "civilization of Indians." [19] These residential
schools were operated by private organizations, mainly missionary societies, with subsidies from the federal government.
Gradually the government took over direct operation of these
facilities. The twentieth-century variation on this sad and destructive theme is the boarding schools of the U.S. Bureau of
Indian Affairs, nearly 100 of which were still in operation in
1965. Bremner, after reviewing the government's efforts concerning the education of Indian children, concludes that "the
broad impact of institutions under government control or influence on children of minority groups was to enforce an alien
way of life and a degrading conception of themselves, incompatible with growth and fulfillment." [20]

Efforts to conquer the minds of Indian youth were not always overtly oppressive. A more subtle and humane attempt
to "civilize the infidel savages" is reflected in the establishment during the seventeenth century of preparatory boarding
schools for Indians at Harvard College in Massachusetts [21]
and at the College of William and Mary in Virginia.[22] Dart-
mouth College was established in 1754 as an "Indian Charity
School" by the Reverend Eleazar Wheelock. It was transferred in 1769 from Lebanon, Connecticut, to its present cam-
pus in New Hampshire. When it failed to attract Indian
youngsters,[23] it was gradually transformed into a college for
European settlers. Harvard and the College of William and
Mary were also unsuccessful in attracting Indian youth and
eventually relinquished these missionary efforts.

Another important type of residential institution for children and youth originated in colonial times to serve educational and socialization needs of top and upper-middle social strata. A study of private schools of colonial Boston mentions several tutors who established boarding schools in their homes for sons and daughters of wealthy families and instructed them in classical and modern languages, mathematics, sciences, and religious teachings.[24] Residential grammar and preparatory schools were established also in conjunction with the early institutions of higher learning, including Harvard College, soon after 1636,[25] and the College of William and Mary, early in the eighteenth century.[26] Several prestigious boarding schools were established in the eighteenth and nineteenth centuries: Governor Dumner Academy, 1763; Phillips Academy, 1778; Phillips Exeter Academy, 1781; Lawrence Academy, 1793; Mercensburg Academy, 1836; Groton School, 1884; The Ursuline Academy for Girls, 1727; the Moravian Seminary for Girls, 1742; and Abbot Academy for Girls, 1829.[27] At present the number of private boarding schools on the elementary and secondary level throughout the United States exceeds several hundred. Comprehensive guides are published annually to help wealthy families in selecting boarding schools suited to the needs of their children.[28] Private boarding schools pride themselves on their graduates' high rate of college admission, especially to the private high-prestige universities. With racial and social class integration in public schools, increased enrollment in private boarding schools may be expected as a way of protecting the exclusive and segregated socialization process of upper-middle-class youngsters.

A third type of institutional care, the evolution of which is traceable to prerevolutionary days, is residential settings dealing with a variety of circumstances regarded as being outside the range of normalcy. These include orphanhood,

abandonment, illegitimacy; serious physical and mental disabilities; behavioral patterns defined as undesirable, such as
laziness, vagrancy, and truancy; and various parental inca-
pacities. Such circumstances were more likely to result in
placement when associated with destitution.[29] Such institutions came into widespread use only in the nineteenth century. In earlier days such children shared institutional facilities with adults. These facilities, known as almshouses, or
workhouses, provided shelter for the entire range of "surplus"
populations, irrespective of sex, age, and type or cause of dependency.

The care of dependent children in almshouses was considered progressive and humane during the latter half of the
eighteenth century. Prior to that time, dependent children
were often auctioned off to the highest bidder ready to pay
for the right to keep and exploit them; or they were "inden-
tured" or "bound out" by the courts to farmers, craftsmen, or
tradesmen who considered them a source of cheap labor.
Even after the widespread adoption of the poorhouse system,
children continued to be bound out as soon as they were old
enough to work for their keep. Humane considerations no
doubt played a part in arrangements for the care of dependent children. The historical record suggests, however, that
efforts to economize carried a decisive weight in public
choices about children who were, after all, only the offspring
of "inferior segments" of the population.

During the nineteenth century, the public became concerned with the conditions of children vegetating in almshouses. Charitable and religious organizations established institutions for the care of orphans and other dependent
children, as well as for the physically handicapped, the mentally retarded, and juvenile delinquents. Gradually, also, state
legislatures realized the shocking conditions of children in
public poorhouses and provided support to privately oper-

ated institutions. When this method of subsidy proved inadequate, states, counties, and municipalities began to erect their own child care institutions. Simultaneously, laws were enacted in state after state requiring removal of children from the poorhouses and placement in specialized children's institutions.

The nineteenth century was a century of institution building. Social reformers promoted a wide range of theories concerning the redemptive potential of highly structured institutional living.[30] However, public enthusiasm and support were eventually followed by disappointment when exaggerated claims remained unfulfilled. Furthermore, in spite of the allocation of public funds to child care facilities, they usually operated on quite limited budgets. The ideas of reform-minded designers and administrators were thus never fully implemented and tested. Consequently, by the end of the nineteenth century, child care institutions were once more viewed as failures. The stage was set for several decades of heated debate between defenders of institutional care and opponents who advocated foster family care or even care of "dependent" children in their own families.[31]

The controversy still continues and has been reflected in child welfare literature throughout the twentieth century. By now, extreme positions for and against institutional care have become more flexible. Kadushin has summarized prevailing thinking as follows:

Child welfare workers developed a hierarchy of preferences in making decisions regarding what was most desirable for the child: the child's own home, even if inadequate in many respects, was felt to be better than the best boarding home; a boarding home, even if inadequate in many respects, was felt to be better than the best institution. More recently, however, the controversy regarding the relative merits of the boarding home and the institution has been redefined in different terms. The institution is no longer viewed in terms of a hierarchy of preferences but, rather, in terms of its appropriateness for certain groups of children who cannot be served by any other kind of facility. Institutions and boarding homes are currently seen as complementary, rather than competitive, resources. Each is necessary and appropriate for different groups of children, and each has a particular place in the total pattern of child care services.[32]

But throughout the long and often bitter controversy about different means of child care, little consideration has been given to the most crucial variables in terms of eventual outcome. These are the social function, the definition of the social context, and the developmental expectations implicit in that definition, of a child care system. Let us turn to these questions.

SOCIAL FUNCTION OF RESIDENTIAL CHILDREN'S INSTITUTIONS

All residential children's institutions may be understood as means of socialization. Their general function is to aid in the preparation of children for their eventual roles as adults. Children's institutions are thus important components of a society's stratification system. Different social strata tend to evolve different preparatory processes and experiences. It is therefore not surprising that residential children's institutions vary in relation to the statuses and roles for which they serve as preparation and that admission is not random, but is controlled by rigid criteria.

The three types of children's institutions reviewed in the preceding section—boarding schools for American Indian children, private boarding schools for children from affluent families, and institutions for dependent children—reflect different specializations within the overall socialization function. Each institutional type was developed to carry out unique societal functions, and its social context has been defined accordingly. Likewise, expectations concerning the adult statuses and roles of children brought up in these institutions vary considerably.

Since early days, the objective of institutions for Indian children has been to undermine the indigenous cultures of these tribes, to destroy their own socialization processes, and to acculturate children to the alien lifestyles that surround them. Tribal cultures were defined in these schools as "primitive" and "savage," while the white man's culture was presented as intrinsically superior. Indian children were induced to believe themselves and their tribes to be inferior, uncivilized, and underdeveloped. At the same time, they were not encouraged to enter white American society as equals. They were expected, instead, to return to their tribes and become exponents of the racist ideology of their arrogant though, at times, well-intentioned oppressors.

The function of private boarding schools for children whose families belong to the social, professional, economic, and political elites of the nation is very different. Built into the fabric of these preparatory schools is the expectation that students will move on to prestigious colleges and will eventually achieve positions of leadership and power. These institutions then serve as conveyor belts, or escalators, for children who are "programmed to succeed" by criteria of the dominant culture, and to fill superior statuses. Access tends to be selective and is controlled largely by the simple mechanism of tuition fees. The more prestigious a school, the more selective and restrictive its admission policies tend to be.

The social context and function of residential institutions for dependent children is defined differently. Just as the expectation of social success has been built into the very fabric of private boarding schools, so the expectation and acceptance of failure or, at best, mediocrity has been built into institutions for dependent, neglected, and delinquent children.[33] The history of these institutions here and in Europe reveals a constant function, irrespective of changes in structure, administration, professional theories, or labels. Statements from well-intentioned child welfare administrators, professionals, community leaders, and politicians notwithstanding, this function has been to "process" lower-income and dependent children into inferior or deviant social and economic statuses and roles as adults; and to do so at least possible cost to the public treasury.[34]

We see now the significance of the failure of the census to define private residential schools as "institutions," excluding their children from the enumeration of "inmates of institutions," while residents of institutions for dependent, neglected, and delinquent children are included.[35] The former group are said to be excluded because these children have a "usual residence elsewhere," but of course most dependent, neglected, and delinquent children have also a "usual residence elsewhere." To justify this inconsistency, the Census Bureau cites the "demand for statistics" on the part of health and welfare administrators and social scientists, an argument that merely seems to beg the question. It does reveal, however, that the biases of administrators and social scientists help to decide who is defined in and out of the usually stigmatizing category "inmate of institutions." In truth, statistical information on children in private boarding schools would be needed for somewhat the same purposes as information on residents in child welfare institutions. The real, yet covert, reason for treating children in private boarding schools differently in the census seems to be that the privileged and affluent are entitled to privacy, and their affairs are not to become "statistics." These children are defined as normal, even though they are in institutional care. Poorer children are not entitled to the same privacy, and their affairs are subjected to public scrutiny and scientific analysis.

A striking differentiation between the two types of institutions is absence of professional and theoretical linkages between them. These facilities are usually not inspected, licensed, and accredited by the same agencies. Their staff members rarely belong to the same professional organizations, do not attend the same conferences, are not trained in the same disciplines and schools, and do not share common educational and psychological theories. It was observed earlier that an extensive survey of child welfare institutions did not trouble to secure background data on the children or on the objectives of the institutions. If these two systems are to be kept apart, how convenient that we should not have to know *what* is being kept apart!

The differences seem very revealing. Child welfare specialists working with dependent children have for decades maintained that institutional placement of children is intrinsically harmful and should be avoided. This view, which was never shared by the private boarding schools, was based primarily on a set of vague psychological concepts, for example, "separation trauma," and "maternal deprivation." These complex phenomena were blamed for a variety of undesirable side effects and consequences of institutional placement.[36] Yet children in private schools thrived and seemed to be relatively immune to these dangers. No doubt, the radically different social context and expectations of private schools must have neutralized whatever negative forces were operating in institutional living, and the boarding schools were thus able to continue processing generation after generation of social elites. Similar evidence concerning the crucial importance of the definition of the social context for the eventual outcome of institutional placement is available from Great Britain's Public Schools and from children's houses in Israeli Kibbutzim.

The constructive experiences of many children in congregate educational settings in the United States and other countries support the hypothesis that there are no intrinsically
destructive aspects in child care institutions. Such institutions
are essentially neutral tools which may be used constructively
or destructively, depending on the particular mix of social,
economic, educational, and psychological ingredients. If their
social purpose derives from egalitarian and humanistic values
and, hence, is aimed at maximizing every child's inherent
developmental potential, and if economic provisions and educational and psychological measures match that purpose, then
children will thrive in the setting. If, on the other hand, the
social purpose reflects a nonegalitarian, discriminatory, and
punitive philosophy, and if economic, educational, and psychological measures match that purpose, then children are
likely to be thwarted in their development. This proposition
brings us to the all-important issue of the value premises
underlying the programs of our various children's institutions.

VALUE PREMISES AND IDEOLOGIES

It is now possible to identify the value premises, ideologies,
and theoretical positions that shape the dynamics and the
professional practice in residential child care. The implicit
view seems to be that children from different segments of society are of different intrinsic worth. Indian children are
worth less than children of middle-class white families, and
children dependent on the public for support are worth less
than children from families who pay their own way.

In brief, social inequality seems to be part of the brick and
mortar of our children's institutions. To put it bluntly may
shock devoted child welfare practitioners and administrators

and may strike them as slanderous. After all, Americans pride themselves on being an egalitarian, democratic, and child-centered society. Yet in spite of our ritualistic commitments to, and sincere yearnings for, an egalitarian social order, inequalities are thoroughly structured into the fabric of our society.[37] Our system of residential child care has never been, nor is it today, an exception. Humanistic and egalitarian values have been reflected here and there, yet their influence has never had a dominant effect.

The ideology of social inequality is reflected today in such concepts as the "indigenous culture of poverty." [38] These concepts underlie theoretical positions that shape our social services—including child welfare services and social reforms such as the war on poverty,[39] and the Model Cities Program.[40] The central theoretical theme is that poor persons are responsible for their own state.[41] Hence, it is they who need to be changed rather than the social order and its premises of inequality, competition, and rugged individualism.

The premises and theories are reflected prominently in the socialization processes of residential children's institutions. As we have seen, they are geared to maintain social stratification. Private boarding schools prepare children of elite groups for creativity and leadership and elite positions. Boarding schools for children of Indian tribes and child welfare institutions prepare their charges for "adaptation" and "adjustment" and inferior statuses.

LIFE IN RESIDENTIAL
CHILDREN'S INSTITUTIONS

What is life like for children residing in various types of children's institutions? This important question cannot be answered reliably, for systematic national information about the quality of children's experience in residential institutions has never been collected.

Several reports on life in institutions have been published by professionals working in the institutions, by social scientists observing them, and also by former inmates.[42] Such studies are unusual, and institutions engaging in them may not be representative. On the other hand, muckraking reports on scandalous conditions in children's institutions which, every now and then, make headline news may also not represent general conditions. All that is attempted here is to deduce qualitative aspects from available quantitative data of one national study.

Perhaps the most significant criterion of the quality of life of institutional children is the extent to which an institution's milieu facilitates individuation rather than regimentation. Actualization of every child's developmented potential and human worth—the professed goal of child welfare services—requires that children be individualized in interaction with truly caring adults, adults who respect them, hold out standards for their development, and stimulate self-respect and aspirations in the children. And the objective of child development requires that children have the material and symbolic resources necessary for realizing these expectations. To what extent do conditions in our children's institutions permit this kind of individuation? The 1966 census of children's institutions [43] may throw light on this question.

During 1965 over half the children residing in public and charitable institutions were living in institutions caring for more than 100 children, nearly one-third in institutions with over 250 children, and over 12 percent in institutions with more than 500 children. Institutions caring for delinquent children tend to be large, whereas institutions for emotionally disturbed children tend to be smaller.[44] To the extent that bigness suggests regimentation, the majority of children must have suffered from it.

The way institutional staffs perceive their children is important, because, however valid, it is a real aspect of the children's milieu. In 1966, staffs in child welfare institutions judged that three out of four children were emotionally disturbed or exhibited disordered behavior.[45] This would require a broad scope of individual attention, not to mention treatment. Prior to admission, nearly all children received physical examinations, 70 percent had dental checkups, 56 percent were tested by psychologists, and 31 percent were evaluated by psychiatrists. But only 18 percent of children admitted to institutions for the neglected and dependent and 35 percent of children entering institutions for delinquents were evaluated psychiatrically.[46]

The primary treatment strategy for children in institutions is individual therapy or counseling by psychiatrists, psychologists, and social workers.[47] However, only 6 percent of all children received regular treatment from psychiatrists during 1965. Most of these children were in psychiatric inpatient units and institutions for emotionally disturbed children. In institutions for dependent and neglected children, less than 3 percent received psychiatric treatment, and in institutions for delinquents such treatment was provided to less than 6 percent. Treatment by social workers—a very vague term indeed —was available in 1965 to 42 percent of all institutionalized children. In institutions for dependent and neglected children 32 percent were receiving social work treatment, while in institutions for delinquents nearly 50 percent received such treatment. Individual counseling or treatment by psychologists, chaplains, probation-parole workers, physicians, psychiatric nurses, and others was provided to 15 percent of all children in institutions.[48]

Two-thirds of school-aged children living in institutions attend schools operated by the institutions, while one-third go to regular community public schools. Attendance at public

schools is especially low for children in institutions for delinquent children, about 5 percent, while 60 percent of children
in institutions for the dependent and neglected go to public
school.[49] Separate educational facilities may result in isolation of children and may have negative effects on their self-
image. Rarely does such separate education mean better education, although at times separate, specialized education is
geared to the unique needs of children in institutions.

Children in institutions are likely to require special help
with their academic studies. Only 17 percent of all children
in institutions receive individual tutoring. Among delinquent
children the need for such help may be greatest. Only 15 percent of children in institutions for delinquents receive individual tutoring.[50] These low percentages raise serious questions concerning the "individuation" goal and suggest that
children's institutions tend to have low aspirations for the
academic achievement of inmates. Getting by with a C seems
to be considered success. Twenty-seven percent of children in
institutions participated in "remedial education." In institutions for dependent and neglected children less than 20 percent benefited from remedial education, while 35 percent received such educational aid in institutions for delinquents.[51]

The encouragement of special interests and talents of children is a meaningful indicator. Nearly half the institutions
have no programs whatsoever in art, music, creative dancing,
and so forth and less than 40 percent of all institutionalized
children are reported to take part in such programs.[52] Programs for physical education are not available at all in 45
percent of the institutions, and 65 percent of children are said
to participate. In institutions for dependent and neglected
children 54 percent participate in physical education.[53]

Is low emphasis on academic studies accounted for by a
strong emphasis on vocational education? Less than 31 percent of all children in institutions and less than 21 percent in

institutions for dependent and neglected children participated in vocational training, while half the children in institutions for delinquents received some vocational training. Six-
ty-four percent of all institutions had no programs available
for vocational training.[54]

In 1965, there were 161 social workers, 82 teachers, 58 psychiatrists and psychologists, 126 physicians and dentists, and
132 other professionals for every thousand children. There
were 192 full-time and 68 part-time child care workers per
thousand children. Institutions for dependent and neglected
children had 134 full-time child care workers per thousand
children; institutions for delinquents had 181.[55] Directors of
nearly half of all public and charitable children's institutions
had graduate degrees. The proportion of graduate degree
holders was lower among directors of institutions for dependent and neglected children (39 percent) and institutions for
delinquent children (42 percent). Fourteen percent of all institutions had directors without a college degree, and 10 percent had directors with only a high school education or less.
In over half the institutions employing social workers, these
positions were held by workers lacking a graduate degree.
About one-third of all the institutions did not employ social
workers.

Fifty-six percent of the institutions had no minimum educational requirements whatsoever for child care staff. This proportion was higher in institutions for neglected and dependent children (65 percent), but lower in institutions serving
delinquent children (48 percent). Indeed, 17 percent of the
institutions had child care staff who had never attended high
school. Eleven percent of institutions for delinquent children
had child care workers who had not even finished grammar
school.

The poor educational level of child care staff has frequently been commented upon; yet progress seems unimpres-

sive. In few public and charitable children's institutions in
the United States are child care workers considered as professional colleagues, a status to which many of them aspire and
which has been attained in some European countries. The
limited education of child care workers tends to be reflected
in low salaries, low social prestige, high turnover, and, worst
of all, low morale. Men and women who work with children
of low social status are treated as if they too were of little
worth. The implicit attitudes are not conducive to enhancing
the development of the children. Because child care staff
serve as role models for the children, the children's aspirations
are in turn depressed. Thwarted themselves, child care workers are, by and large, ill-equipped to stimulate children toward creativity and self-actualization. As a reaction, moreover, child care staff are often embroiled in severe conflicts
with professional co-workers. These conflicts are known to
obstruct treatment efforts of some of the most sophisticated
institutions.[56]

Because of the staffing patterns sketched above, child care
tends to deteriorate in many institutions into emphasis on
routines, discipline and chores—a custodial milieu that lacks
imagination, joy of living, and constructive stimulation. The
emphasis on obedience and discipline is often reflected in punitive and manipulative approaches that involve also the use
of cruel and violent measures. At the same time, a chronic
problem of underfinancing leads to overcrowding and a de-
teriorating physical environment.[57]

We conclude with judgments obtained from the directors of
the institutions themselves. In the directors' collective judgment, they cared for about 70,000 children who would have
been better off elsewhere. That is, at least one in three children should not have been retained in those institutions. In
the same year, ironically, the directors had to reject, for lack
of space, staff, or facilities, some 55,000 children whose needs,

they thought, could have been matched in their institutions.[58]

The directors' collective judgment implies an answer to the question whether existing children's institutions facilitate optimal development. The answer seems to be "no." If the directors themselves feel they are not meeting the needs of one in three children, then something in the institutional system must be terribly wrong.

The quality of life in an institution is not necessarily determined by specific details, although details are important, but rather by underlying attitudes and values. The details are merely functions or indicators of these underlying attitudes and values. From the details reviewed here, we can only assume that children in the main receive custodial care—care that does not facilitate individuation or child development.

No systematic information is available on the quality of life and education in private boarding schools. It may be suggested that attitudes and values implicit in the milieu of private boarding schools are likely to be much more conducive to individuation and self-actualization of children than in public and charitable institutions. This assumption is supported by evidence reflected in the results of the two institutional systems.

CONCLUSIONS

The social policies underlying institutional care for dependent, neglected, and delinquent children seem to be conducive to low-quality ameliorative services. The potential impact of these services on structural causes of dependency, neglect, and delinquency seems worse than naught. These programs not only fail to attack causes, but actually perpetuate them by processing children for adult positions of low social status and limited rights. In other words, public and charitable residential institutions maintain inequalities intact and fail to equip graduates to participate equally in civil, political, social, and economic rights and responsibilities.

In concluding, I should like to reemphasize that residential child care can operate to achieve constructive and liberative objectives as well as destructive and oppressive ones. The use to which private boarding schools are put demonstrates this. Our child welfare institutions could be transformed into channels for equality, freedom, and creativity if, and when, we redefine their social purpose in these terms. To achieve this requires a broad commitment to the intrinsic and equal worth of every child. Such a commitment would remove built-in obstacles in the operation of our child welfare institutions. We would then establish a single child care system, specialized according to children's needs rather than their social background. We could be guided in this quest by John Dewey's dictum, "What the best and wisest parent wants for his own child, that must the community want for all of its children." [59] We have the professional, scientific, technological, and economic capacity to carry out such a radical reform of our children's institutions. What has been lacking to activate this capacity is the political will. It is time we face up to this simple truth.

NOTES

1. David G. Gil, *Unravelling Social Policy—Theory, Analysis, and Political Action Toward Social Equality* (Cambridge, Mass.: Schenkman Publishing Co., 1973).
2. *Profiles of Children,* 1970 White House Conference on Children (Washington, D.C.: Government Printing Office, 1970), p. 147, Table 107.

3. Seth Low, *America's Children and Youth in Institutions 1950–1960–1964*, U.S. Department of Health, Education, and Welfare, Children's Bureau (Washington, D.C.: Government Printing Office, 1965), p. 31, Table 2.
4. Low, *America's Children*, p. 32, Table 3.
5. Low, *America's Children*, p. 2.
6. U.S. Bureau of the Census, *Statistical Abstract of the United States: 1971* (Washington, D.C.: Government Printing Office, 1971), p. 23, Table 21.
7. Donnell M. Pappenfort, Dee Morgan Kilpatrick, and Alma M. Kuby, *A Census of Children's Residential Institutions in the United States, Puerto Rico, and the Virgin Islands: 1966*, 7 vols. (Chicago: The University of Chicago, The School of Social Service Administration, Social Service monographs, 2d ser., 1970).
8. Shirley A. Star and Alma M. Kuby, *Number and Kinds of Children's Residential Institutions in the United States*, U.S. Department of Health, Education, and Welfare, Children's Bureau (Washington, D.C.: Government Printing Office, 1967).
9. Bernard Greenblatt, ed., "Residential Group Care Facilities for Children," in *State and Local Public Facility Needs and Financing, Study Prepared for the Subcommittee on Economic Progress*, Joint Economic Committee, 89th Cong., 2d sess. (Washington, D.C.: Government Printing Office, 1967), see especially section on "User Charges," pp. 633–634.
10. Low, *America's Children*, p. 8.
11. Low, *America's Children*, pp. 8–9.
12. Low, *America's Children*, p. 9.
13. Low, *America's Children*, p. 9.
14. Low, *America's Children*, p. 10.
15. Alfred Kadushin, *Child Welfare Services* (New York: Macmillan, 1967), p. 528. Reprinted by permission of Macmillan Publishing Co., Inc. from *Child Welfare Services* by Alfred Kadushin. Copyright © 1967 by Alfred Kadushin. See also Henry S. Maas and Richard E. Engler, Jr., *Children in Need of Parents* (New York: Columbia University Press, 1959); Shirley Jenkins and Mignon Sauber, *Paths to Child Placement* (New York: Community Council of Greater New York, 1966).
16. Kadushin's three quotes are from U.S. Congress, Senate, *Hearings before the Public Health, Education, Welfare and Safety Subcommittee on the District of Columbia*, 89th Cong., 1st sess., May 10, 1965 (Washington, D.C.: Government Printing Office, 1965).
17. Robert H. Bremner, ed., *Children and Youth in America, A*

Documentary History, Vol. 1, 1600–1865 (Cambridge, Mass.: Harvard University Press, 1970), p. 74.

18. Bremner, *Children and Youth in America, Vol. 1*, pp. 74–75.
19. Bremner, *Children and Youth in America, Vol. 1*, pp. 438–439, 547–558.
20. Bremner, *Children and Youth in America, Vol. 1*, p. 439. This quote refers to Indian and also to black children.
21. Bremner, *Children and Youth in America, Vol. 1*, p. 72.
22. Bremner, *Children and Youth in America, Vol. 1*, pp. 76–78.
23. Bremner, *Children and Youth in America, Vol. 1*, pp. 319–322.
24. Robert Francis Seybolt, *The Private Schools of Colonial Boston* (Westport, Conn.: Greenwood Press, 1970), pp. 11–13, 16, 17, 24, 29, 32, 34–37, 40, 41, 43, 44, 49, 52, 57.
25. Bremner, *Children and Youth in America, Vol. 1*, p. 85.
26. Bremner, *Children and Youth in America, Vol. 1*, pp. 91–93.
27. Clarence E. Lovejoy, *Lovejoy's Preparatory School Guide* (New York: Simon and Schuster, 1971).
28. See for instance Porter Sargent, *The Handbook of Private Schools—An Annual Descriptive Survey of Independent Education*, 52nd ed. (Boston, Mass.: Porter Sargent, 1971). *Private Independent Schools—The American Private Schools for Boys and Girls* (Wallingford, Conn.: Bunting and Lyon, Inc., Publishers, 1971); Lovejoy, *Lovejoy's Preparatory School Guide; The Vincent Curtis Educational Register* (Boston, Mass.: Vincent Curtis Educational Register, published annually).
29. For more detailed historical information on institutional care for dependent children, readers should consult Bremner, *Children and Youth in America, Vol. 1*, pt. 1, chap. 3; pt. 2, chap. 4; pt. 3, chap. 5; *Vol. 2*, pt. 3; "Child Welfare: Institutions for Children," in *Encyclopedia of Social Work*, vol. 1, ed. Robert Morris et al. (New York: National Association of Social Workers, 1971), pp. 120–128; Kadushin, *Child Welfare Services*, pp. 518–521.
30. David J. Rothman, *The Discovery of the Asylum—Social Order and Disorder in the New Republic* (Boston: Little, Brown, 1971).
31. Martin Wollins and Irving Piliavin, *Institution or Foster Family—A Century of Debate* (New York: Child Welfare League of America, 1964).
32. Kadushin, *Child Welfare Services*, pp. 520–521. Quoted by permission of Macmillan Publishing Co., Inc.
33. Alexander Liazos, "Processing for Unfitness—Socialization of 'Emotionally Disturbed' Lower-Class Boys Into the Mass Society" (unpublished Ph.D. diss., Brandeis University, 1970).

34. For a historical perspective on residential institutions for dependent children see Bremner, *Children and Youth in America*. For a recent journalistic exposition of conditions in
residential children's institutions which reflect the built-in expectation and acceptance of failure see Howard James, *Children in Trouble—A National Scandal* (New York: David
McKay, 1970).
35. Low, *America's Children*, Appendix A, Census Definitions and
Explanations, pp. 25–29.
36. John Bowlby, *Maternal Care and Mental Health* (Geneva,
Switzerland: World Health Organization, 1951); *Deprivation
of Maternal Care—A Reassessment of its Effects* (Geneva,
Switzerland: World Health Organization, 1962); *Maternal De-
privation* (New York: Child Welfare League of America,
1962).
37. David G. Gil, "Some Thoughts on Social Equality" (Waltham,
Mass: Brandeis University, 1972). Unpublished.
38. Oskar Lewis, *The Study of Slum Culture—Backgrounds for La
Vida* (New York: Random House, 1968); Edward C. Banfield,
The Unheavenly City (Boston: Little, Brown, 1970); Edward
C. Banfield, "The Cities: The Lower Class," *New York Times*,
October 12, 1970; Richard Todd, "A Theory of the Lower
Class," *The Atlantic*, September 1970.
39. Stephen M. Rose, *The Betrayal of the Poor, The Transforma-
tion of Community Action* (Cambridge, Mass.: Schenkman
Publishing Co., 1972).
40. Roland Warren, "The Model Cities Program—An Assessment,"
in *The Social Welfare Forum, 1971* (New York and London:
Columbia University Press, 1971).
41. William Ryan, *Blaming the Victim* (New York: Pantheon
Books, 1971).
42. See for instance Howard W. Polsky, *Cottage Six* (New York:
Russell Sage Foundation, 1962); Lydia F. Hylton, *The Residential Treatment Center, Children, Programs, and Costs*
(New York: Child Welfare League of America, 1964); Rosemary Dinnage and M. L. Kellmer Pringle, *Residential Child
Care—Facts and Fallacies* (New York: Humanities Press,
1967); Liazos, "Processing for Unfitness."
43. Pappenfort *et al.*, *Census*.
44. Pappenfort *et al.*, *Census*, p. 33, Table 24.
45. Pappenfort *et al.*, *Census*, p. 53, Table 42.
46. Pappenfort *et al.*, *Census*, p. 81, Table 70; p. 85, Table 74; p.
89, Table 78; p. 93, Table 82.
47. Kadushin, *Child Welfare Services*, p. 535.

48. Pappenfort *et al.*, *Census*, p. 97, Table 86; p. 101, Table 90; p. 105, Table 94.
49. Pappenfort *et al.*, *Census*, p. 127, Table 114.
50. Pappenfort *et al.*, *Census*, p. 137, Table 124.
51. Pappenfort *et al.*, *Census*, p. 141, Table 128.
52. Pappenfort *et al.*, *Census*, p. 147, Table 134; p. 149, Table 136.
53. Pappenfort *et al.*, *Census*, p. 155, Table 142; p. 157, Table 144.
54. Pappenfort *et al.*, *Census*, p. 151, Table 138; p. 153, Table 140.
55. For details see Pappenfort *et al.*, *Census*, pp. 166–229, Tables 153–216.
56. Polsky, *Cottage Six;* Irving Piliavin, "Conflict Between Cottage Parents and Caseworkers," *Social Service Review*, 37 (March 1963).
57. James, *Children in Trouble.*
58. Pappenfort *et al.*, *Census*, pp. 238–245, Tables 225–232.
59. Quoted in James K. Whittaker, "Group Care for Children: Guidelines for Planning," *Social Work*, 17, no. 1 (January 1972), 60.

4

Day Care for Whom?

ARTHUR C. EMLEN

Federal support for day care has arisen in times of national emergency—the Civil War, the Great Depression, World War II. Day care released manpower for the war effort; after each crisis, the crash program was allowed to expire. Recently, we have been witnessing a new spending of federal moneys for day care to help toward the employment of parents receiving public welfare and to provide compensatory education for disadvantaged children. Interest in day care has burgeoned, and new horizons for child development have come into view.

Important forces have joined to create a broad day care movement going beyond the war on poverty and giving it more universal scope and purpose. The extent of maternal employment gave day care a degree of universality as maternal employment increased until one-third of the mothers of preschoolers and half of the mothers of school-agers could be found working. Research encouraged a period of experimentation and openness to the potentials of day care, as the effects of maternal employment were not by themselves found to be unfavorable.[1] Day care and equal employment opportunities for mothers were promoted by Women's Liberation as a right, and the concept of comprehensive day care became a shibboleth of liberal politics.

Still, a really major expansion of day care has failed to take place. After less than a decade, the war on poverty is winding down, and day care threatens to become an instrument—a weapon—to get families off welfare. Organized day care serves less than 10 percent of the children of working mothers, and disadvantaged children, despite their priority, are not reached in substantially greater proportion. Day care, as we know it, is inappropriate for the majority of those who are supposed to need it. Day care has been conceived in such a way that it cannot be funded, nor delivered, nor used on a large scale. At the same time, very little effort has been spent to strengthen the kinds of child care arrangements that most families use and prefer.

This chapter takes stock of the state of day care.[2] What is its extent and who has been reached? How has need been determined? How does day care fit into the life of a child and his family? Has day care been appropriate for welfare families? What needs have not been met? Day care literature has been full of optimism and excitement, as well as alarming chronicles of need. The purpose of this chapter is to analyze the nature of the need critically, particularly in relation to the disadvantaged.

THE EXTENT OF EXISTING DAY CARE

Day care developed as a form of child placement in out-of-home settings supervised by social agencies. Day care was not originally regarded as a resource for any customer, but rather was a comprehensive professional service for families

TABLE 4-1

Federal Spending for Day Care and Other Early Childhood
Programs—Fiscal Years 1970–1973 (Millions of Dollars)

Program	1970	1971	1972 (Estimate)	1973 (Estimate)
Day care	164	233	404	507
Head Start	330	363	364	369
Preschool programs under Elementary and Secondary Education Act, Title 1	26	92	98	93
Total	520	688	866	969

SOURCE: Charles L. Schultze *et al.*, *Setting National Priorities: The 1973
Budget* (Washington, D.C.: The Brookings Institution, 1972), Table 8–1,
p. 253. Used by permission of Charles L. Schultze of The Brookings Institution. Day care data for 1970 are from *Child Data and Materials*, Senate
Committee on Finance, 92 Cong., 1st sess., 1971, p. 32; other 1970 data
are from *Special Analyses, Budget of the United States Government, Fiscal
Year 1972*, pp. 120–21; all other data are from *Special Analyses, Budget
of the United States Government, Fiscal Year 1973*, pp. 123, 144.

and children under special stress. With the advent of Head
Start, day care became more educational in philosophy. In
the end, it emerged as an omnibus program of child care, education, nutrition and health care, social services, and parent
participation.

Following the inception of Head Start in 1965, federal
funds were committed to day care through a variety of programs: Work Incentive Program (WIN), Concentrated Em-
ployment Program (CEP), Aid to Families with Dependent
Children (AFDC), Child Welfare Services (CWS), Head Start
(Summer, Half-day, Full-day), Parent Child Centers, Model
Cities, Aid to Educationally Deprived Children in Low-In-
come Families, Assistance for Migrant and Seasonal Farm
Workers, Assistance for Handicapped Children, Food Ser-
vices, Health Service Migrant Health, Preschool and School
Health Program, Foster Grandparents, Training Educational
Professions.[3]

The estimated federal level of support between 1970 and 1973 ranged from half a billion to slightly under one billion dollars a year (see Table 4–1). That these figures are modest should not obscure the fact that the nation embarked upon a subsidized day care program. The lion's share went to AFDC families and to Head Start, though most of Head Start funds went for half-day programs. In 1971 nearly a quarter billion dollars was spent for full-day day care to serve an estimated 440,000 children.[4]

The most dramatic fact about day care services is the small proportion of children they accommodate. In 1971 the children of working mothers numbered nearly 6 million under the age of 6 and 18 million between 6 and 14. Rough estimates of the potential day care populations are provided by Parker and Knitzer:[5]

Potential Day Care Population	Number of Children under 6
Physically and emotionally handicapped	2.0 million
Economically disadvantaged	3.3 million
Working mothers	5.8 million

The 440,000 children who received full-day day care are a small proportion, even of the economically disadvantaged group.

The most recent national child care survey that sampled families with incomes under $8,000 was conducted by the Westinghouse and Westat Corporations.[6] They found approximately 10 percent of preschool children of working mothers in day care centers with seven or more children (see Table 4–2). Three-fifths of the centers were proprietary, and only about one center in four was providing "developmental care" —education and a range of other services. In addition, less than half of one percent of the children from low- and modest-income families were in *licensed* family day care arrangements (19 percent were in family day care homes of which 2 percent were licensed).[6]

The only large-scale day care institution operating in the United States is the private, informal arrangement at home or in other family homes (see Table 4–2). Those who provide this type of day care are fathers, siblings, relatives, housekeepers, friends, and neighbors. Ninety percent of preschool children of working mothers are in arrangements of this kind. Children of working mothers are more apt to be cared for in their own homes than out of home, and twice as many are cared for in the home of a nonrelative than in a day care center of any kind—public, voluntary agency, or proprietary. The child care arrangements used by AFDC recipients are closely representative of the proportions for working mothers generally.[7]

The largest increase from 1965 to 1970 was in the percentage of mothers who worked exclusively during school hours. The largest decrease was in children for whom no special care could be reported. Conceivably, opportunities for part-time work are serving to protect more children of working mothers than community facilities of any sort.

We have seen how small a percentage of the target population has been reached by day care facilities. The other institutional alternative, which is to license care in family homes, has also been of little effectiveness. Moreover, the quality of day care centers appears not to be greatly influenced by licensing. Welfare agencies were not prepared when Congress required them in 1962 to certify all homes in which welfare recipients placed their children. Since 1968, when federal requirements finally emerged, agencies have fretted over standards that can be realistically applied and nevertheless protect all or most children. The net effect has been to sidetrack

TABLE 4–2

Percentage Distribution of Child Care Arrangements of Working Mothers, by Age of Children—1965 and 1970

| | AGE OF CHILDREN | | | |
| | Under 6 Years | | 6 to 14 Years | |
Child Care Arrangement	1965°	1970†	1965°	1970†
Care in own home	48.0	49.9	66.0	78.7
By father	14.4	18.4	15.1	10.6
By other relative	17.5	18.9	22.6	20.6
By a nonrelative	15.3	7.3	6.8	4.5
Mother worked during child's school hours	0.8	5.2	21.5	42.9
Care in someone else's home	30.7	34.5	9.2	12.6
By a relative	14.9	15.5	4.7	7.6
By a nonrelative	15.8	19.0	4.5	5.0
Day care center	5.6	10.5	0.6	0.6
No special care ‡	15.7	5.0	24.3	8.3
Total	100.0	100.0	100.0	100.0

SOURCE: Charles L. Schultze *et al.*, *Setting National Priorities: The 1973 Budget* (Washington, D.C.: The Brookings Institution, 1972), p. 261. Used by permission of Charles L. Schultze of The Brookings Institution. Data for 1965 are from Seth Low and Pearl G. Spindler, *Child Care Arrangements of Working Mothers in the United States*, U.S. Children's Bureau and U.S. Women's Bureau, 1968, pp. 15, 71; Westinghouse Learning Corporation and Westat Research, Inc., "Day Care Survey—1970: Summary Report and Basic Analysis," prepared for Evaluation Division, Office of Economic Opportunity (1971; processed), pp. 175, 178–180. Figures are rounded and may not add to totals.
° When several kinds of care were used for the same child, the predominating and most recent child care arrangement is given.
† Child care arrangements on the last day the mother worked.
‡ Includes child looked after self, mother looked after child while working, and other.

staff from regulating the relatively few but serious abuses where they might have had an effect.

The history of licensing reveals that it does not so much add new resources as it changes the respectability of old ones. Doubling the licensed homes has made but a small contribution. And consider the question of quality. Developmental care facilities have an average ratio of 1 caregiver to 6 children; the others, though licensed, have an average ratio of 1 to 14.[8] By contrast, unlicensed family day care homes have an average caregiver-child ratio of 1 to 3, *including* the caregiver's own preschool children.[9] In other words, being licensed tends to mean that a day care arrangement includes too many children. A recent national survey of quality of care, while without merit in its sampling, does document the dismal quality in proprietary facilities despite licensing.[10]

THE NEED AND DIFFICULTIES

The state of the art of determining need is primitive. It has concentrated on estimating need for centers rather than for services across all settings. The criteria have led to inflated estimates of effective demand for center care, while serious obstacles to expansion have been treated as trivial.

Informal, unofficial arrangements are not regarded as day care by the professional establishment. Therefore, all of the children who are not in licensed facilities have been counted as part of the need. For example:

Experts agree . . . that all the existing services for children meet no more than 10% to 15% of the need. Some of the facts that lend credence to this dismal estimate include . . . *Neglect*—The nation's working mothers alone have 11 million children under twelve years of age. But there are fewer than ½ million places in licensed day care centers across the country.[11]

But formal licensed care is not necessarily of higher quality than unlicensed care. Day care of good quality is not necessarily a solution for urgent problems such as neglect and abuse. And it is unlikely that the present users of informal care would prefer, and would switch to, formal facilities if available.[12] The difficulty is that formal day care is not a convenient solution for many mothers. We shall return to this point.

Waiting lists, overenrollment, and underenrollment figures have been used to provide a crude measure of demand, but they reflect distribution problems more than need. Free services and high-quality centers are apt to have waiting lists, but if there existed enough conveniently located day care centers to saturate the demand for this type of resource, then underenrollment probably would be endemic, keeping their financing shaky.

Expressions of dissatisfaction and preference are a third type of indicator that has widely been represented as suggesting more need than a cautious reading would support. For example, the Westinghouse-Westat report shows that "358,000 low-income families are very dissatisfied with their present arrangements for child care." [13] But most mothers report being *satisfied* with the type of care that they are using.[14] Moreover, day care center users are also dissatisfied; none of the available options for day care is necessarily preferred.[15]

Among working mothers, the largest preference is to stay home—a point conspicuously overlooked in estimates of need for day care. Two conclusions are suggested about measures of dissatisfaction. First, other alternatives may be preferred to day care by those who are dissatisfied—a children's allowance, for example, or some other respectable alternative to working. And second, dissatisfaction may be expressed even when people will not change. Solemn and straightforward conversion of dissatisfaction into need for facilities is highly misleading.

Finally some cautions are in order in interpreting the claims of widespread need for day care that are based on demographic projections. 1. Although the absolute numbers may increase, the proportions using formal types of day care are not likely to change radically. 2. Improved economic conditions for young families may reduce maternal employment and demand for full-time day care. 3. Universal extension of kindergartens and half-day preschool programs could reduce the demand for full-day care. 4. The "baby bust" or declining birth rate has already decreased the base rates of demand. The 1970 census shows three million fewer children under five than there were in 1960, despite the largest increase yet among women of childbearing ages.[16]

Though the reader might welcome a reasonable estimate of need at this point, the answer is not available. Unfortunately, the right questions have not been asked. In any event, day care has not expanded in any way resembling real need, let alone the need that some have seen. An examination of why begins with an appreciation of the confusion and conflict over the goals of day care. The Comprehensive Child Development Act that was vetoed by the president in 1971 was intended to create a complete package of services in organized and subsidized facilities. Debate centered around the cost of developmental versus custodial care; even government estimates for custodial care, while less than the $2,000 proposed by many legislators, are so expensive as to create a major political issue. Choices must be made even among the children of working mothers, of AFDC recipients, of the poor, or physically or emotionally handicapped children. In the public debate about these choices, one perceives that it is not clear whether the object is to reduce welfare rolls, to overcome poverty, to remedy the effects of disadvantage in child development, to promote optimum child development, to prevent child neglect, to compensate for lack of resources in households with only one parent, to benefit families of all working mothers, to implement equal occupational opportunity for women, or to encourage womanpower in selected occupations.

Day care is a political issue among its current and potential consumers as well. Brookings analyst Alice Rivlin describes the results as "a rather erratic two-class system in which *some* poor children (those fortunate enough to get into the subsidized centers) get better care than is available to families with somewhat higher incomes. The mother with income slightly above the poverty line has the worst deal of all. . . ." [17] The desirability of subsidized day care programs has whetted the appetite for benefits among persons who are ineligible for them on the basis of family income. How much taxpayer support will there be for day care for others among families in which wives do not work, and how much support for day care for the poor will there be among the not quite so poor?

A second problem, neatly called the "prime sponsor" issue in legislative debates, involves a host of thorny questions of funding, delivery, and monitoring of quality day care. How would parent participation and community control be implemented? What would be the roles of the federal government, of states, of cities, and of neighborhood groups? How would day care services be coordinated? Who would take responsibility for the development of a comprehensive range of day care services?

A Federal Panel on Early Childhood had to be created to plan across government departments involved in financing day care. A similar local body was needed to manage "cross-funding" from diverse federal sources for an integrated local program. Many of these so-called 4-C Councils facilitated the movement of funds for day care, but localities still reflect the lack of coordination and planning at higher administrative levels.

A third obstacle to expansion of day care is the lack of

trained personnel. The government's Office of Child Development (OCD) has been especially concerned to avoid expansion that would be inadequately staffed and would "warehouse" young children. Jule Sugarman, former OCD chief and a strong supporter of day care, cautioned legislators as follows:

> I have concluded that our capacity for program growth in kindergarten, nurseries and day care programs (combined) is roughly 250,000 children per year. Growth beyond that level does not seem feasible in terms of our potential resources. Therefore, it appears that given adequate funds, it will be at least twenty-four years before the program growth model can be completed.[18]

Vested interests—both providers and consumers—have presented a fourth problem in the development of day care. Minority groups have been sensitive to the possibility of yet another "rip off" at their expense. Robert Hess has noted intense dissatisfaction among poverty program and welfare rights groups and a consequent belief that it is futile to cooperate with government programs.[19] Private entrepreneurs have created national anxiety about the quality of care; at the same time they have used their influence to undermine day care under community auspices.[20] Likewise, universities, consulting firms, agencies, and professions vie to fill the expected professional vacuum. One suspects that the overwhelming bias of professionals in favor of the day care center —in contrast with family or informal care—represents a vested interest. Only the organized facility offers the professional direct control.

The problem of professional stake in these programs is not readily resolved. Social work, education, and health have all made significant contributions to center-based programs. Yet early childhood programs no longer fit easily into any existing professional-institutional framework. Social work has been more geared to case-by-case service than to a large-scale or preventive system. Education has too often been at a loss to deal with parents or other programs. Even if a new professional amalgam were to coalesce, it would risk competing with the family. Conflict between the family and professional institutions is perhaps more latent than manifest, and is expressed by failure to use facilities or by alternation between delegation and jealous exercise of parental control.

Finally, some awareness of the gaps in our knowledge is in order, because they constitute one obstacle to expansion of day care. In the late 1950s and early 1960s during a period of interest in maternal separation and institutional deprivation, a number of investigators assessed the effects of maternal employment and thus, as a corollary, of some form of day care. Maternal employment by itself was not found to affect the child's adjustment.[21] To some extent this dispelled apprehensions about day care, but opened up the need for further work on more sensitive outcome measures, on the type of day care, and on pivotal parental attitudes, family variables, and socioeconomic conditions. Especially, effects of day care on the development of infants and toddlers remained to be studied. For example, will day care programs interfere with the attachment tendencies of infants at a critical developmental period so as to create a later incapacity for close relationships? [22]

In the second half of the 1960s came enthusiasm for compensatory intervention. This was to take place in day care centers, Head Start programs, and in demonstration facilities, with a heavy emphasis on curricula that would improve cognitive abilities. Home care and family day care tended to be ignored,[23] and the decade ended without comparing the effects of formal and informal settings. Head Start could point to many successes in the area of health [24] and community action,[25] but a complicated and equivocal picture resulted with respect to compensating for handicaps.[26]

In late 1971, OCD sponsored a review of day care research.[27] Two excerpts are especially relevant:

Issues Relating to Children. There have been a few evaluation studies of day care programs which describe the impact of particular, exceptional programs on children but the variety of programs and the great number of possible effects make it difficult to draw inferences about the impact of "typical" day care programs on children. The Chapman and Lazar (1971) summary draws special attention to the impact of certain features of day care; e.g., separation from mother, changes within and between programs, mixtures of various ages, social and ethnic groups, and family, educational or experiential backgrounds. The previous studies have tended to assess the effects of day care on children's physical and cognitive development. The more subtle, social-emotional variables, which are probably most directly related to the day care experience, have gone unassessed. This gap in available evidence is probably best attributed to the difficulty of conceptualizing and measuring these variables (e.g., trust, independence, self-concept, achievement motivation, happiness) but the area is a critical one for day care research.[28]

Support Services in Day Care Programs. Support services, including provision of medical, dental and mental health services, nutrition and social service, have been present to some extent in most day care centers and systems. Present and proposed Federal programs have increased the emphasis given to these support programs for low income families. Little is known, however, about their effectiveness, and virtually nothing has been done to show how the needs of the vast majority of children, those cared for in their own homes or in family day care arrangements, can be assessed and met. Perhaps the single largest need for demonstrations is the provision of comprehensive, cost-effective service to children in the non-licensed, mother-arranged settings.[29]

FAMILIES ON WELFARE

Nowhere is the problem of determining need more evident than with AFDC recipients referred to work incentive (WIN) programs. Despite evidence to the contrary, the belief persists that new day care slots will get families off welfare.

Assessing the role of day care in WIN, Steiner shows that up to February 1970, 22,000 welfare recipients were employed out of 1.5 million screened by local agencies for possible referral [30]—that is 1.5 percent. The 22,000 employed represent only 7 percent of those regarded as employable, and 17 percent of those enrolled in the WIN program.

It has been popular to point to lack of day care facilities as the major obstacle to "workfare" employment. A Department of Labor report says, "Lack of child care is the most serious barrier for any employment program involving mothers." [31] Yet this factor shrinks in significance among considerations such as poor education and job skills, lack of employment experience, and the absence of placement opportunities. Recent studies of WIN place major responsibility for program failure upon the lack of available jobs, a lack that trainees know about during training and that affects their attitude throughout.[32] A longitudinal study of WIN dropouts reported in 1972 by Franklin concluded that: "Difficulties with child care and transportation are often mentioned as barriers to employment. In the third interview our data . . . show that these were not important considerations for continuing in the program." [33]

A powerful determinant of the type of child care arrangement used is family size. Of the children of working mothers who require care, almost half are in arrangements in their own homes when one child is involved and three out of four are in their own homes when four or more children are involved.[34] Obviously, cost and convenience lead the large family especially to avoid out-of-home day care of any kind. Indeed, only one in ten working mothers has four or more children. But one-third of AFDC families have four or more children, and another 18 percent have three children.[35] One has to give some thought to the feat of management that is asked of a mother who is to work and dispose of three or four children in day care centers, not to mention the cost to her or someone, to grasp how frivolous it is to regard formal day care as a solution to her problem.

One may also consult mothers' preferences. Westinghouse-Westat surveyed low-income households in which the mothers were *not* working. "Not interested in working," "cannot find job," and "prefer not to work while children are young" accounted for 61 percent of the responses.[36] Only one in five responses suggested that the mother might work if day care were available or the family could afford it. One observes that while many mothers work, many do not—particularly when they have young children at home. In the interest of sound policy it may be well to recognize both patterns.

Even leaving preference aside, however, formal day care appears to be much inflated as a support for work for the AFDC population. Indeed, most WIN enrollees make informal arrangements with family, friends, or others. In this, as it happens, they are like all working mothers.

HOW DO INFORMAL DAY CARE ARRANGEMENTS FIT INTO THE LIVES OF CHILDREN AND FAMILIES?

The moral of the welfare story is that day care must fit into family life before it can serve other objectives. It is unrealistic to expect the poor to perform feats of consumer behavior that others cannot or will not. We have noted the prevalence of informal, private family day care. Perhaps it would be well to understand why.

First, family day care is economical and convenient for one or two children, but not for large families; patterns of use reflect this, with 70 percent of arrangements involving one child under 6.[37] (In this, however, it is similar to all forms of out-

of-home care.) Whites use family day care disproportionately
—42 percent versus 23 percent for blacks in one survey.[38]
White-collar workers pay more for such care than blue-collar
or service workers; and whites pay more than blacks. It is no
surprise that those who can pay more use family day care;
those who cannot pay rely perforce on relatives or other free
service.

Second, family day care accommodates children of any age
and accommodates all the children in a family—preschoolers
and older children after school. However, it "specializes" in
the youngest children. Two-thirds of the children of working
mothers are of school age, but two-thirds of the children in
family day care are under 6.[39] The young family of these
working mothers finds a complementary fit with the somewhat older family of the caregiver who completes her partially empty nest with day care children.[40]

Third, family day care minimizes the strain of distance and
transportation time. One study found three out of four arrangements within one mile of home. Beneath this statistic
lies a relationship that Zipf calls the "principle of least
effort": [41] the cumulative percentage of arrangements increases as the logarithm of the distance.[42]

Fourth, family day care affords a nearby, familiar situation,
with the parent in charge and readily able to participate,
plus a tolerable delegation of authority without threat to parental feelings.[43]

Fifth, use of this type of care reflects for some a desire to
avoid the use of relatives. In many families with relatives not
available, it seems in any event to be more acceptable than a
center.[44]

It is generally viewed with satisfaction by those who use it
and those who provide it.[45] Despite strains inherent in this
arrangement, caregivers and users tend to believe it works
well for the child.[46] Investigators have not found this confi-

dence very often misplaced, although developmental effects have not been investigated. The quality of care is probably similar to care received in the users' own homes.

Studies of private, unlicensed family day care have been conducted in Spokane,[47] Portland,[48] Pasadena,[49] and New York City.[50] All report the caregivers as generally nurturant and capable women. The New York results differ in two respects—finding care in substandard housing and a user preference for center care. The New York City sample was largely black and Puerto Rican, and the center care preference appears to be attributable to the poor housing and neighborhood conditions. (The design of the study introduced a sampling bias as well by studying center applicants.)

Briefly, what can be said about the quality of family day care? The caregiver is apt to be mature, experienced, capable, warm, nurturant, and relatively child oriented. Her motivations tend to involve a modest degree of economic need and a considerable expressive need to be caring for children.[51] Typically, she cares for only a few children [52]—an overriding fact that carries related benefits. It affords availability, individualization, and responsiveness to the affective needs and cognitive interests of the child, comparing favorably with the typical day care center.[53] It provides new learning and socialization experiences, including cross-age associations the child would not have at home.

On the other hand, caregivers may vary widely in their motivations, capabilities, and talents for child rearing; in some families, the language stimulation and social and emotional benefits may be limited. Cases of exploitation, neglect, and abuse do occur, though relatively infrequently, as do instances of unsafe housing, poor health conditions, and inadequate situations for play. And some family day care arrangements lack stability and result in discontinuity of care.

Family day care now competes in magnitude with the use

of relatives both in the home and out of the home; and twice as many preschool children are found in family day care as in center care of any kind. A new substitute for kin has quietly emerged. Like the extended family, it has strengths and weaknesses. Nevertheless, private family day care, like other types of informal child care, clearly has a firm foundation in consumer demand and a natural feasibility. As a silent, large-scale, unsupervised demonstration project for approximately 1.2 million preschool children, it rates pretty high marks. Its weaknesses call for supportive services that have yet to be developed.

WILL THE REAL DAY CARE NEEDS
PLEASE STAND UP?

Once freed of tunnel vision in which only centers appear, we can focus on other day care needs as well. We have seen that the use of home care and family day care cannot be counted as part of the need for center care, because each type of day care is likely to be used by families of different stages, sizes, and compositions, as well as by people with different preferences and social experiences. The need is not for creating new facilities so much as for improving the use of existing resources. Careful diagnosis of day care needs will lead us to develop a system of solutions, some of which will involve specialized use of formal facilities, some will involve supportive services for strengthening informal care, while others will involve policy changes that go far beyond the usual scope of day care programming.

For example, many day care consumers do experience difficulty in *finding* child care even when there is no lack of resources, but the need is for systems of information and referral.[54] Discontinuity of care besets children in child care arrangements of all kinds, but it occurs mostly because care users move their residence, change jobs, or experience other dislocations of family life that require stabilizing forces beyond what day care can provide.[55] Day care is a factor (though its importance has been exaggerated) in job absenteeism and turnover, but the answer lies less with industrial day care centers, which can be used only by a small proportion of employees, than with information and referral services as well as with shorter hours and flexible work schedules for mothers who carry special responsibilities for family life.[56] There are "latch key" children who look after themselves after school, but opportunities for part-time maternal employment may contribute more than services to a large-scale solution.[57] Neglect and abuse do occur, but they are not easily reached, and they remain largely untouched by formal day care programs.[58] Informal child care arrangements do take place in unsafe, substandard housing,[59] but such basic socioeconomic conditions are not corrected by licensing programs nor are they circumventable in substantial numbers by subsidized home improvement or recruitment to centers.

Finally, some children suffer developmental and educational handicaps which Head Start is designed to remedy. However, Head Start reaches but 20 percent of its target population, and despite important contributions, remedial efforts can expect limited effects without much broader changes in family and neighborhood life, in the level of child-rearing culture, and in the social and economic structure of society.[60]

We have examined how the stage was set for a day care expansion that has not materialized. The obstacles were many and fundamental, the prevailing conception of need exaggerated and misdiagnosed.

America was asking the wrong question. It was asking, "How many day care facilities should we create?" when it should have been asking, "How can we expand and improve the patterns of child care that families are already using?" It also should have been asking, "What kinds of preventive policies can we devise to reduce the rates of other problems for which day care is an inadequate solution?"

In a society designed to strengthen the ability of parents to raise their children, what shape should day care take? We would provide child development centers, but they would serve more children for shorter hours. For full-time care, informal arrangements in family homes would be relied upon without disparagement and under favorable conditions. Informal care would be reinforced by natural systems of social and technical assistance, and information services would be provided to all families and caregivers. There would be a system of policies and services to improve the quality of family, neighborhood, and community life. Finally, there would be basic economic support for young families, so as not to drive mothers to work before their families are ready.

The shape of day care today lacks such comprehensive effort. We see independent day care worlds: fine developmental centers for a limited number of the poor and disadvantaged, and no services at all for the majority of the disadvantaged, nor especially for those at the margin between poverty and ability to pay. Indeed, at all levels, families using proprietary centers, informal neighborhood care, or their own homes receive no attention.

After all the talk about disadvantaged children, how can day care wind up so poorly distributed? Can the narrow focus on providing quality care in centers—which never will be provided because of a shortage of manpower and financing—be functional? There is a great appearance of helping poor women to work when they cannot, will not, and perhaps should not. Meanwhile, the day care needs of those who do work are misdiagnosed, and the services that could be provided are not.

NOTES

1. See Elizabeth Herzog, *Children of Working Mothers*, U.S. Department of Health, Education, and Welfare, Children's Bureau (Washington, D.C.: Government Printing Office, 1960); Lois Meek Stolz, "Effects of Maternal Employment on Children: Evidence from Research," *Child Development*, 31 (December 1960), 749–782; Bettye M. Caldwell, "The Effects of Infant Care" in *Review of Child Development Research*, ed. Martin L. and Lois W. Hoffman (New York: Russell Sage, 1964); F. Ivan Nye and Lois Wladis Hoffman, *The Employed Mother in America* (Chicago: Rand McNally, 1963); *On Rearing Infants and Young Children in Institutions*, Children's Bureau Research Reports no. 1 (Washington, D.C., 1967).

2. Original research reported here, the Field Study of the Neighborhood Family Day Care System, was a project of the Tri-County Community Council in cooperation with Portland State University, and was financed by research grant no. r–287 of the U.S. Children's Bureau, Office of Child Development.

3. Listing taken from Ronald K. Parker and Jane Knitzer, "Day Care and Preschool Services: Trends in the 1960's and Issues for the 1970's," in *Government Research on the Problems of Children and Youth: Background Papers Prepared for the 1970–71 White House Conference on Children and Youth* (Washington, D.C.: Government Printing Office, 1971), pp. 263–267. These programs represent several separate pieces of legislation, such as Title IV-A of the Social Security Act (as amended, 1967); Titles I-B, II, and III-B Economic Opportunity Act, 1964; Title I, Demonstration Cities and Metropolitan Development Act, 1966; Title I, Elementary and Secondary Education Act, 1965; Handicapped Children's Early Educational Assistance Act, 1968; National School Lunch Act (as amended, 1968).

4. Parker and Knitzer, "Day Care and Preschool Services," p. 254.

5. Parker and Knitzer, "Day Care and Preschool Services," p. 202.

6. Jody R. Johns et al., *Day Care Survey, 1970* (Bladensburg, Md.: Westinghouse Learning Corporation and Westat Research, Inc., 1971).

7. Charles L. Schultze et al., *Setting National Priorities: The 1973 Budget* (Washington, D.C.: The Brookings Institution, 1972), p. 268.

8. Schultze *et al.*, *Setting National Priorities*, p. 264.
9. Arthur C. Emlen, Betty A. Donoghue, and Rolfe LaForge, *Child Care by Kith: A Study of the Family Day Care Relationships of Working Mothers and Neighborhood Caregivers* (Corvallis, Oreg.: DCE Books, 1971), p. 69; Johns, *Day Care Survey, 1970*.
10. Mary Dublin Keyserling, *Windows on Day Care* (New York: National Council of Jewish Women, 1972).
11. *Fact Sheet*, Day Care and Child Development Council of America, Washington, D.C., 1968.
12. Arthur C. Emlen, "Realistic Planning for the Day Care Consumer," in *Social Work Practice 1970* (New York: Columbia University Press, 1970), pp. 127–142.
13. Johns *et al.*, *Day Care Survey, 1970*, p. XIX.
14. Johns *et al.*, *Day Care Survey, 1970*, p. 127.
15. Arthur C. Emlen, Betty A. Donoghue, and Quentin D. Clarkson, *The Stability of the Family Day Care Arrangement: A Longitudinal Study* (Corvallis, Oreg.: DCE Books, 1973).
16. George Grier, *The Baby Bust* (Washington, D.C.: Washington Center for Metropolitan Studies, 1971).
17. "Day Care: Policy Questions for an Expensive Program," *Washington Post*, March 5, 1972.
18. *Senate Hearings on S. 1512, Comprehensive Child Development Act of 1971* (Washington, D.C.: Government Printing Office, 1971), p. 292.
19. Robert Hess, "Parent-Training Programs and Community Involvement in Day Care," in *Day Care: Resources for Decisions*, ed. Edith H. Grotberg (Washington, D.C.: Office of Economic Opportunity, 1971), pp. 300–301.
20. Elizabeth Prescott *et al.*, *An Institutional Analysis of Day Care* (Pasadena, Calif.: Pacific Oaks College, 1971).
21. See Herzog, *Children of Working Mothers;* Stolz, "Effects of Maternal Employment"; Caldwell, "Effects of Infant Care"; Nye and Hoffman, *The Employed Mother*.
22. Attachment and related aspects of socioemotional development are a complex area of investigation that has hardly been explored in relation to day care. See, for example, the review by Irving E. Sigel *et al.*, "Social and Emotional Development of Young Children," in *Day Care: Resources for Decisions*, ed. Grotberg, pp. 109–134.
23. See, for example, Grotberg, *Day Care: Resources for Decisions*, and Edith H. Grotberg, ed., *Critical Issues in Research Related to Disadvantaged Children* (Princeton, N.J.: Educational Testing Service, 1969). Exceptions may be found in the

work of Susan Grey at Peabody College, Ira Gordon in Florida, Phyllis Levenstein in New York, Nancy Travis in the southeastern United States, Camille Wade in Milwaukee, Wisconsin, June Sale in Pasadena, California, and the author and his associates in Portland, Oregon, to cite some recent examples.

24. Gertrude T. Hunter, "Health Care Through Head Start," *Children,* 17, no. 4 (July–August 1970), 149–153.

25. Lois-Ellen Datta, "Head Start's Influence on Community Change," *Children,* 17, no. 5 (September–October 1970), 193–195.

26. Grotberg, *Critical Issues.*

27. Judith E. Chapman and Joyce B. Lazar, *A Review of the Present Status and Future Needs in Day Care Research,* prepared for the Interagency Panel on Early Childhood Research and Development, November 1971; and Thelma Zener, "OCD Research Priorities," Research and Evaluation Division, Office of Child Development.

28. Zener, "OCD Research Priorities," pp. 2–3.

29. Zener, "OCD Research Priorities," pp. 2–3.

30. Gilbert Y. Steiner, *The State of Welfare* (Washington, D.C.: The Brookings Institution, 1971), p. 73.

31. Keyserling, *Windows,* p. 16.

32. David S. Franklin, *A Longitudinal Study of WIN Dropouts: Programming and Policy Implications* (Los Angeles: Regional Research Institute in Social Welfare, 1972); Ronald E. Fine, *et al., Final Report—AFDC Employment and Referral Guidelines* (Minneapolis: Institute for Interdisciplinary Studies, 1972).

33. Franklin, *WIN Dropouts,* p. 175.

34. Figures regrouped and percentaged from Seth Low and Pearl G. Spindler, *Child Care Arrangements of Working Mothers in the United States* (Washington, D.C.: Government Printing Office, 1968), p. 83.

35. AFDC figures taken from Steiner, *State of Welfare,* p. 41; full-time working mother figures from Low and Spindler, *Child Care Arrangements,* p. 51.

36. Johns *et al., Day Care Survey, 1970,* p. 174.

37. Emlen *et al., Child Care by Kith,* pp. 53–54.

38. Herbert S. Parnes *et al., Years for Decision: A Longitudinal Study of the Educational and Labor Market Experience of Young Women,* Manpower Research Monograph No. 24 (Washington, D.C.: Government Printing Office, 1971), pp. 132–140. Percentages were based on number reporting necessity of making regular arrangements.

39. Low and Spindler, *Child Care Arrangements;* see comparison in Arthur C. Emlen and Eunice L. Watson, *Matchmaking in Neighborhood Family Day Care: A Descriptive Study of the Day Care Neighbor Service* (Corvallis, Oreg.: DCE Books, 1970), p. 57.
40. Emlen *et al., Child Care by Kith,* p. 49 and chap. 5.
41. Emlen *et al., Child Care by Kith,* pp. 59–62; George K. Zipf, *Human Behavior and the Principle of Least Effort* (New York: Hafner, 1949, 1965).
42. Emlen *et al., Child Care by Kith,* p. 61.
43. Emlen *et al., Child Care by Kith,* pp. 109–110.
44. Emlen *et al., Child Care by Kith,* pp. 62–65.
45. Emlen *et al., Child Care by Kith,* pp. 107–109, 188.
46. Emlen *et al., Child Care by Kith,* chaps. 8 and 9.
47. Joseph B. Perry, "The Mother Substitutes of Employed Mothers: An Exploratory Inquiry," *Marriage and Family Living,* 23 (November 1961), 362–367; also see chapters by Perry and Nye in Nye and Hoffman *Employed Mother in America.*
48. Field Study of the Neighborhood Family Day Care System, reported upon in Emlen, *et al., Child Care by Kith.*
49. June S. Sale with Yolanda L. Torres, *"I'm Not Just a Babysitter": A Descriptive Report of the Community Family Day Care Project* (Pasadena, Calif.: Pacific Oaks College, 1971).
50. Elizabeth Vernon and Milton Willner, *Magnitude and Scope of Family Day Care Problems in New York City* (New York: Medical and Health Research Association of New York City, 1966); Milton Willner, "Unsupervised Family Day Care in New York City," *Child Welfare,* 48, no. 6 (June 1969), 342–347; Milton Willner, "Family Day Care: An Escape from Poverty," *Social Work,* 16, no. 2 (April 1971), 30–35.
51. Emlen *et al., Child Care by Kith,* chap. 5.
52. Emlen *et al., Child Care by Kith;* 1.6 day care children, according to the Westinghouse-Westat survey, Johns *et al., Day Care Survey, 1970,* pp. 6, 97, 201.
53. Elizabeth Prescott, "Group and Family Day Care: A Comparative Assessment," in *Family Day Care West: A Working Conference* (Pasadena, Calif.: Pacific Oaks College, 1972).
54. Alice H. Collins and Eunice L. Watson, *The Day Care Neighbor Service: A Handbook for the Organization and Operation of a New Approach to Family Day Care* (Portland, Oreg.: Tri-County Community Council, 1969); Emlen and Watson, *Matchmaking;* Arthur C. Emlen, "Slogans, Slots, and Slander: The Myth of Day Care Need," *American Journal of Orthopsychiatry* (in press); Alice H. Collins, "Natural Delivery Systems:

Accessible Sources of Power for Mental Health," *American Journal of Orthopsychiatry*, 43 (January 1973), 46–52.

55. Emlen *et al.*, *The Stability of the Family Day Care Arrangement*.

56. Johns *et al.*, *Day Care Survey, 1970*, pp. 159, 173; for an example of troubles, see David F. Hawkins *et al.*, *Industry Related Day Care: The KLH Child Development Center, Part I* (undated); for an example of a more successful alternative, see "Illinois Bell Day Care Referral Made Permanent Because of Savings and Improved Company Relations," *Day Care and Child Development Reports*, vol. 1, no. 8 (1972). For a promotional review of industry day care, see Department of Labor Bulletin 296, *Day Care Services: Industry's Involvement* (Washington, D.C.: Government Printing Office, 1971). The Portland study found that a number of issues relating to the hours the child is in care were associated with role strain and emotional drain for family day care caregivers, Emlen *et al.*, *Child Care by Kith*, chap. 9. See also Betty A. Donoghue, "What Do Mothers and Caregivers Want in a Family Day Care Arrangement?" in *Family Day Care West*.

57. Emlen *et al.*, *The Stability of the Family Day Care Arrangement*; Emlen and Watson, *Matchmaking*.

58. Emlen and Watson, *Matchmaking*; Alice H. Collins, "The Home-Centered Woman as a Potential Protective Service Resource" (paper presented to the National Conference on Social Welfare, Dallas, Tex., 1971).

59. Willner, *Child Welfare*.

60. *Report on Preschool Education* (Washington, D.C.: Capitol Publications, February 23, 1972); Grotberg, *Day Care: Resources for Decisions*, p. 276; Jerome Hellmuth, ed., *Disadvantaged Child*, vol. 3, *Compensatory Education: A National Debate* (New York: Brunner/Mazel, 1970).

5

AFDC as
Child Welfare

GEORGE HOSHINO

A discussion of child welfare would be incomplete without a consideration of income maintenance programs. These provide protection against contingencies that interrupt income or create the need for additional income. Among these contingencies are old age and retirement, unemployment, illness and disability, death of the breadwinner, family breakup, and large family size.

In an industrial society the great majority of families normally depend on earned income for sustenance and amenities. Assurance of an adequate and steady flow of cash income is, therefore, critical. Consequently, all modern nations have an impressive array of cash benefit schemes that benefit children. These include the social insurances such as unemployment compensation and Old Age, Survivors, and Disability Insurance (OASDI); various demogrant or flat pension schemes such as the children's allowance programs of Britain and France and, indeed, of every major country except the United States; and public assistance.

This discussion is devoted to public assistance and specifically to the category of Aid to Families with Dependent Children (AFDC) provided for under the federal Social Security Act. AFDC is the program relied upon to care for the most needy of the nation's children. For them and the adults who care for them it is literally the last bulwark against destitution. As of June 1971, there were 10.2 million recipients of AFDC in 2.7 million families which included 7.4 million children.[1] Of a total of $8.4 billion spent in 1970 for all categories of public assistance, $4.9 billion was for AFDC. During the 1960s the number of recipients of, and expenditures for, AFDC rose precipitously. Only 3.1 million individuals (2.4 million children) were receiving AFDC as of December 1960, and expenditures for money payments in 1960 totaled $1.0 billion; as of December 1965, the figures were 4.4 million recipients (3.3 million children) and $1.6 billion.

The percentage of the nation's children under age 18 who were dependent on AFDC increased proportionately, reaching 10.7 percent in June 1971. Of these children, 46 percent were Negro and 45 percent white. The remainder were American Indian and other racial minorities. Families go in and out of AFDC at a rapid rate. Therefore AFDC touches a greater proportion of the nation's children than the June 1971 figure indicates. Of all children reaching age 18 in 1963, it was estimated that 15.9 percent, about one out of six, had been on AFDC at some time.[2] The current proportion probably is over 20 percent. Probably, at least three out of five black children reaching age 18 have received AFDC at some time. The only public institution with greater impact on the nation's children may be public schools. At the same time, more than in other welfare programs, AFDC is expected to provide various kinds of personal and community social services. This purpose was made explicit by Congress with amendments to the Social Security Act in 1962 and 1967.

With such goals, expenditures, and scope, how well does AFDC provide for children and what social policy for children does it express? We look first to the nature of the AFDC program, the benefits and services provided, and conditions governing their receipt.

PUBLIC WELFARE

Public assistance is characterized by the following basic features, each of which has crucial consequences for the program and children:

1. State responsibility for program auspice and administration.
2. Federal participation through a system of open-end grants-in-aid to the states for specified categories of assistance, for example, Medical Assistance (MA), and Aid to Families with Dependent Children (AFDC).
3. Substantial exclusion of the working poor, except as states or localities cover them under nonfederally aided general assistance (GA).
4. Individualized administration of the means-tested money payment by state and local agencies commonly called "welfare departments."
5. Provision of specified social and manpower services in conjunction with, or as a condition of, financial aid.

State responsibility has resulted in violent contrasts and contradictions among the states. Whether a child will qualify at all for assistance, how much he will receive, and whether he and his family will be demeaned and degraded are literally accidents of location. States have wide latitude to establish the conditions of eligibility and the level at which family income will be maintained. Local agencies also have considerable discretion in respect to program administration.[3]

Thus, in some states, no child over 17 can qualify; in others, children up to 21 may if attending school.[4] Cohabitation is grounds for disqualification in some states, but not in others. Stepfathers may or may not be liable for support of stepchildren. Limitations on resources vary widely. In some states the value of the applicant's house is disregarded; other states may require that property valued at more than $2,500 be sold and used for living expenses. The largest amount payable for basic needs to a four-person family ranged from $60 in Mississippi to $349 in Massachusetts per month. Actual monthly average payments per recipient as of July 1971 ranged from $13.75 in Mississippi to $75.83 in New York. In Wyoming, 2.0 percent of the population was receiving AFDC; in the District of Columbia, 10.1 percent.

The wide variations and generally low payment standards can be attributed to the unwillingness or inability of states to finance their programs adequately. On the other hand, the major variations can be attributed to the absence of federal standards in critical areas (for example, no national minimum payment level). And one can criticize federal grant formulas that encourage states to pay less in AFDC than in adult categories. Thus, the Social Security Act provides for federal sharing of AFDC payments up to $32; but in Old Age Assistance (OAA), until the program ended in 1973, up to $75. No wonder states opted for higher OAA grants at the expense of AFDC grants! To maintain children at a level comparable to adult categories greatly increases a state's expenditures and, overall, decreases the federal percentage of reimbursement.

At its inception, AFDC provided only for children whose parents are dead, incapacitated, or absent. It is still for children and parents not normally available for regular employment. In 1961 children of unemployed parents (UP) were included, but with notably restrictive administration. Even so, as of 1970 only 26 states had opted for the new AFDC-UP. AFDC has become largely a program of families headed by women, usually families broken by separation, desertion, or unwed parenthood. Only 18 percent of AFDC families are "normal" families, that is, families composed of a father and mother married to each other and living together in the same home with the children. In 1970, only 5.5 percent of the families were dependent because of the death of the father, 12 percent because of his incapacity, and 5 percent because of his unemployment.

Emphasis on the father's absence is said to encourage fathers to desert and to discourage marriage of unwed parents. Although data from systematic research are limited, doubtless the contention is true in many instances. In any event, present AFDC policy does violate the principle that a family should be economically better off together than separated. Similarly, exclusion of the working poor is criticized on the grounds that the policy is inequitable and discourages work. These criticisms have led to proposals such as a public assistance program in which "need" would be the only requirement of eligibility, the negative income tax, and various forms of the guaranteed annual income covering both the working and nonworking poor. All incorporate some kind of "income disregard" or work incentive provision.

Although the Social Security Act of 1935 was heralded as ending over 300 years of poor-law history in America, the act's public assistance titles, and especially the AFDC title, were to continue that tradition in federal legislation. AFDC is defined as money payments to needy children and their specified caretaker relatives. It is a means-test cash benefit scheme. Although it was assumed that public assistance would "wither away" as the social insurances expanded and the economy improved, such was not to be the case with the children's category. Social insurance has limited capacity to cope with the problem of childhood poverty, and alternative programs in cash or in kind have not been developed. Consequently, rather than becoming the minor supplementary program envisaged, AFDC has become a major and ever-expanding primary maintenance program for a substantial portion of the nation's children.

Welfare, therefore, is big business. The public assistance budget, chiefly for AFDC, is one of the largest items in most state budgets, and welfare departments are among the most controversial of state and local governmental departments. It is in this context that the administration of AFDC and its consequences for children must be seen.

Although there are exceptions, welfare departments serve poor people by and large. Either the means test excludes the nonpoor, as in public assistance and most day care, or only poor families apply, as in child welfare services. A consequence is a "welfare population" and a public image of welfare that reflects its moralistic poor-law heritage. In spite of efforts to extend services more broadly and to change the negative image by adopting titles like "social services" or "family and children's services" public welfare is still public relief in the eyes of most people. "The Welfare," referring to the public welfare agency, and "being on welfare" are the terms used universally by politicians, the general public, newspaper reporters, public welfare staff, poor families, and recipients themselves. These terms reflect the stigma associated with welfare, the slogan "Welfare a Right not a Privilege" notwithstanding.

What is the means test and why is there so much controversy about it? Briefly, the means test is a device for ascertaining whether an individual or family has insufficient means of support; in effect, what does one require and what does one have? If one has less than required he is in need. Theoretically, in a cash benefit scheme, the dollar amount of requirements less the dollar amount of resources equals the amount of the grant. However simple and obvious this formulation may seem in principle it can have painful consequences when put into operation, particularly in a program as large and controversial as AFDC and serving a population in which racial and ethnic minorities and families broken by desertion and unwed parenthood are disproportionately represented.

In addition to defining the population served as a "welfare" population, the means test can have a degrading effect on families. It requires the applicant to declare himself poor, in effect, a failure in an individualistic society that measures success in terms of material wealth. To the agency the applicant must demonstrate his nonpossession of resources sufficient to maintain himself and his family, and the agency must satisfy itself and the public that such is in fact the case. More often than not, the humiliation is compounded by the fact of the application arising out of separation, unwed parenthood, or inability to find work.

The inherently demeaning and deterrent aspects of the means test have been exacerbated in AFDC by the individualized method of determining eligibility for assistance. Early policy makers were convinced that individual determination of need should be built into the new public assistance programs, and social casework theories were applied. However laudable the intent of these policies, the outcome is intricate and confusing requirements, complicated budgeting practices, and detailed investigative procedures that, in the face of hostile public attitudes, are overlaid with a heavy emphasis on deterrence and surveillance.

The issue of whether financial aid should be tied to behavioral requirements or be administered in conjunction with personal social services has not been resolved.[5] A "suitable home" policy, reflecting a fear that public aid would maintain children in homes that endanger them, was adopted by most states and, as Bell points out, has been used to disqualify large numbers of Negro families.[6] Differences of opinion have

always existed as to the nature of the AFDC program—
whether it is a straight financial aid program much like
OASDI, or a form of child welfare to be provided on a social
casework basis. In turn, the premise that social work and rehabilitative services will lead to self-support and a reduction
of dependency tends to conflict with the view of public assistance as a right.

The goal of rehabilitation and self-support was made explicit with the enactment of the 1962 legislation authorizing
social services to recipients, former recipients, and potential
recipients. To encourage state effort, the federal government
pays 75 percent of the cost of such services. Legislation in
1967 created the Work Incentive Program (WIN) to assure
"to the maximum extent possible that each relative, child, and
individual participating in the [AFDC] program will enter the
labor force and accept employment so that he will become
self-sufficient." The 1967 amendments also required states to
unify AFDC social services and child welfare services. Thus,
the policy of attempting to prevent and alleviate poverty and
dependency by focusing on the poor family's personal and social problems and by tying the receipt of financial aid to behavioral conditions and programs of social services and work
was incorporated into federal legislation.

This policy has introduced further confusion, complexity,
and conflict. Probably no governmental program can match
AFDC in its moralistic overtones, capriciousness of administration, and the hostility generated among consumers of service, the agency, and the public. Workers are charged with
policing both program and poor families; at the same time
they are expected to be compassionate and helpful. They are
exhorted to be advocates, but their relationship to their
clients has been defined as investigative and at times adversary by no less than the U.S. Supreme Court.[7] No wonder
workers are unable to do any of these things very well.

Only since the mid-1960s has the principle of individualization been seriously challenged by a movement toward simplification and standardization, flat grants, the use of claimant-completed declarations to determine eligibility, and the separation of financial aid from social services. In spite of these developments, however, AFDC remains basically unchanged at the operating level. The heritage of the poor laws, the complexities of statutory requirements, conflicting purposes, hostile public attitudes, vested interests, and plain resistance to change are barriers to attempts to recast the program into a more simple, efficient, and humane system of administration.

BENEFITS

Of all children who are poor, and thus presumably need assistance, how many are reached by AFDC? In 1970, of the 25.5 million persons below the poverty line ($3,968 for a family of four), 10.5 million were related children under age 18 in families—15 percent of all children under 18.[8] In the same year, an average of 6.2 million children received AFDC. Who are the children denied assistance and, if they are obviously poor, why?

They fall into several broad groups. Most are in families who do not fall into the groups covered by AFDC; they are mainly children of the working poor. Many are in the covered groups and meet the need requirements, but are disqualified by nonneed eligibility requirements. Thousands of families are otherwise eligible, but have incomes just above the low AFDC standards. Finally, thousands more are presumably eligible, but are unaware of their rights to benefits or are deterred from applying. The distribution of families among these broad classifications is not known with any degree of precision. Enough is known, however, to conclude that AFDC does not reach large numbers of poor children. It can be argued that AFDC was never intended to eliminate childhood poverty. Regardless, the AFDC record is discouraging in respect either to the total population of poor children or to the groups for which it is specifically intended.

What can be said of the level of assistance provided by AFDC? By any reasonable criterion of adequacy, the program fails miserably. The Advisory Council on Public Welfare was led to comment that the government itself, by maintaining families at such low levels, was a major contributor to the very poverty upon which it had declared war.[9] Only a few of the highest paying states reach even the modest level of the poverty line. As of July 1971 the monthly payment per recipient averaged only $50.52 nationally. It ranged from $8.27 in Puerto Rico, $13.75 in Mississippi, $15.64 in Alabama, $19.70 in South Carolina, and $20.32 in Louisiana to $75.83 in New York, $74.04 in Hawaii, $71.79 in Minnesota, and $70.38 in New Jersey.

Payments are not the same as the income level at which families are maintained. Many families have earned income (14 percent of recipient mothers work full or part time), support payments by husbands, or social security. In general, however, AFDC families have few additional resources. A 1969 study showed that AFDC families had slightly less than $60 per month of income in addition to the grant.[10]

What does the AFDC payment enable recipient families to get for themselves in the way of food, clothing, shelter, health care, entertainment, and the like? Given the widely varying but low payment levels, it comes as no surprise to find widespread deprivation ranging from a marginal existence in liberal states to extreme deprivation and malnutrition in the lower payment states. A devastating profile is set out in a recently published nationwide study.[11] Thirty percent of urban recipient children and 28 percent of rural recipient children went without milk for a whole day at a time; 3 to 7 percent of children went without food for a whole day at a time. Of city families, one-third had no meat, fish, eggs, or milk products (protein foods) for their main meal on a specified day. One child in eight always or sometimes had to go without lunch. Particularly poignant is the fact that 22 percent of urban and 14 percent of rural recipient children had stayed home from school sometime during the past year because of lack of clothes or shoes.

Other studies portray essentially the same grim picture: a drab, meager existence in which almost all of the income is spent on the bare essentials of life, overcrowded and substandard housing, and inadequate food.

CONSEQUENCES

In dramatic terms, the Report of the President's Commission on Income Maintenance Programs summarizes the effects of poverty on the health of children:

Poor nutrition during pregnancy can hinder fetal brain development and increase the probability of premature birth. Protein deficiencies in early childhood can retard brain growth. This early damage—perhaps followed by frequent illness, further malnutrition, crowded and unsanitary living conditions—is exacerbated by lack of regular medical attention. . . .

The glazed eyes of children, legs that never grew straight, misshapen feet, sallow complexions, lack-luster hair, are easily recognized. . . . Other physical limitations, such as low energy level, are real to poor children in school and adults trying to hold down jobs, but these limitations may be misconstrued by teachers and employers.[12]

These are consequences—opportunity costs, so to speak—of poverty and AFDC policies. Although expenditures for money payments can be stated in precise dollar figures, for the most part the costs of these consequences can be expressed only in descriptive and qualitative terms.

A study of psychiatric impairment among children in the Manhattan area of New York City found that 12 percent of AFDC children had psychiatric disorders, a rate that was three times as high as nonwelfare poor children (4 percent), who had a rate similar to children of higher-income families (5 percent).[13] Mistrustful and anxious personalities were heavily represented among the AFDC children. AFDC children without fathers showed the greatest psychiatric impairment of all children, a finding that would seem to support arguments against policies that exclude fathers and father substitutes. The study concludes, "The problems and handicaps of welfare children do not originate in their low-income status alone."

Public assistance budgets include shelter as a cost item. These allowances are invariably hedged with "reasonable rent" conditions or maximums and often are not kept current; still other rules further reduce the effective amounts of shelter allowances. Like other aspects of AFDC administration, a great deal of discretion rests with workers in respect to moving expenses, furnishings, deposits, and similar items. Therefore, AFDC families, particularly the larger families, are forced to pay out a high proportion of their incomes for substandard housing, reducing the amount of money available for food and other essentials.

Schorr summarizes the effects of poor housing on families with children.[14] Stress accumulates from having constantly to accommodate to others and from lack of privacy. Young children observe adult sexual behavior, and this experience may manifest itself in later sexual problems. Children have higher incidences of infections and childhood diseases, digestive disturbances, and injuries resulting from accidents caused by hazardous conditions. Lead poisoning from swallowing lead-base paint may reach almost epidemic proportions in older central-city slum areas. One reaction of children to over-crowding is simply to stay outside, which effectively cuts them off from their parents and prevents them from studying.

Contrary to public opinion, AFDC families do not stay on the rolls very long, and most never return. The average length of stay is slightly under two years. Many families receive assistance for only a few months, and, to be sure, in some families the parent had been on AFDC as a child. (A 1967 study indicated that 9 percent of mothers and 2 percent of fathers were *known* to have received AFDC as a child, with a large unknown factor.) [15]

Keeping this high turnover rate in mind as well as the fact that AFDC children are young (in 1969 three out of four were age 12 or younger), how are the families situated when they leave AFDC and how do they fare subsequently? Unfortunately, little evidence bears directly on these questions; more longitudinal and follow-up studies are needed.

Of cases closed in the spring of 1961, 34 percent were "still in need but ineligible for AFDC." [16] The distribution by race is significant—29.8 percent of whites and 44.0 percent of Negroes. Of these still-needy cases, a large number were closed for the reason "other," which included a high proportion in two classifications: "Unwilling to comply with agency ruling" (18.2 percent of whites and 21.6 percent of Negroes) and "Unsuitable home, poor moral atmosphere, continued illegal relationship" (23.7 percent of whites and 44.3 percent of Negroes). These data are disturbing in view of the numbers of young children involved and the bias against Negro families.

A 1969 study notes that while families who were no longer recipients were better off than recipients—which would be expected because improvement in financial circumstances is the most frequent reason for terminating assistance—deprivation was still considerable.[17] In fact, only slight improvement is shown on many items; for example, children were still going without milk and protein foods. So the circumstances of families at the time of leaving the rolls or shortly thereafter are still marginal; what about the long-term consequences of the receipt of AFDC?

In a northeastern metropolitan community three groups of families—AFDC recipient families, families who had applied for assistance but been rejected, and families who had neither applied for assistance nor been rejected—were compared in terms of several indicators of social, educational, and behavioral problems displayed by children, for example, school dropout, delinquency, school discipline, aptitude and achievement, and teenage marriage and premarital pregnancy.[18] Of 144 possible instances, AFDC students scored highest on 87. It cannot be said, of course, that AFDC "caused" the problems enumerated, nor can the findings be generalized to all AFDC families. Nevertheless, the data are evidence that AFDC does a poor job of caring for children, and the consequences are costly for them and society over the long run.

AFDC SOCIAL SERVICES

If one considers the "causes" of need for AFDC—death, incapacity, desertion, separation, unwed parenthood, or unemployment—and the problems faced by the poor in general, it seems logical to conclude that AFDC families need help in addition to the money payment. On reflection, however, it is apparent that most families who encounter such crises do not come into AFDC. Most surviving widows and children are assisted by survivors insurance; children of disabled parents, by disability insurance; and temporarily unemployed parents, by unemployment compensation. None of these cash payment schemes is administered in conjunction with social services. In respect to separation, desertion, and unwed parenthood, most families manage on their own, perhaps with the help of relatives and friends or of attorneys, doctors, or ministers. It can be argued that any family may need services in times of crisis, but in fact most do not voluntarily turn to social agencies for help, except for tangible things such as financial aid or day care.

Thus, although AFDC provides social services, there is no reliable way of estimating the need. But a "price of dependency," as O'Neil puts it,[19] is that AFDC families constitute an enormous "captive caseload." This is a premise of the provisions for services and work training and must be kept in mind.

States are required to make available to AFDC families an extensive range of services: protective services to children; child care services such as day care, foster care, and homemaker services; family-planning services and services designed to reduce the number of illegitimate children; family and child counseling and other supportive services intended to enhance family functioning; and health and legal services. States may elect an even wider spectrum of optional services that can include group and community services, and they may extend services to former recipients and potential recipients.

In spite of sizable expenditures ($1.8 billion in fiscal 1971), it is difficult to say just what services have been made available to families and what has been accomplished by them. Statistical data are incomplete, confusing, and conflicting. The basic problem lies in the difficulty of accounting for activities that cannot be described in quantitative terms, a problem not unique to AFDC services.

A 1967 study noted that only small minorities of AFDC families were known to have received services: family planning, just under 20 percent; work or training, 16 percent; referral to vocational rehabilitation, 12 percent; child welfare or crippled children's services, 7 percent.[20] On the other hand, a 1969 survey reported 1.5 million of a total of 1.6 million families as receiving one or more services, mainly related to employment, housing, household management, and health problems.[21] Another report indicated that 832,000 families, including 1.5 million children, were receiving services of some type during December 1969 under the AFDC and child welfare services programs.[22]

These statistics are impressive, but they do not reveal much about the content, quality, or outcome of the services, especially of those designed to "strengthen family life, reduce dependency, and encourage self-support." Despite large efforts and claims, few systematic analyses have been made; those few show little that is positive.

A Wisconsin study indicated that service meant a caseworker visit once every three months for a little more than 30 minutes.[23] There was minimal interaction between worker and recipient, and sensitive areas were avoided. Service activity was described as "little more than a relatively infrequent, pleasant chat." A California study found contacts between workers and recipients to be transient and infrequent.[24] Most recipients viewed their problems in money terms and considered their nonfinancial problems to be bad housing, unemployment, or illness. Services were seen as irrelevant; for example, counseling was given on the problem of bad housing. An atmosphere of distrust and despair was pervasive, and few recipients voluntarily sought help from workers.

A recent New Jersey study found that the service program was mostly a paper operation.[25] Aside from eligibility, most conversations centered on the general upbringing of children, household cleanliness, and the like, rather than on the family's own specific problems. Only 13 percent of mothers reported that a worker had ever offered to help arrange child care to enable them to work, and family planning was seldom touched upon, although these items are emphasized by the 1962 and 1967 amendments. In general, recipients seemed to like the workers, but doubted that they could be of much help.

Two developments might improve the dismal service picture: a recognition that low-income families need and perceive their problems in terms of "hard services" such as housing, health care, and day care instead of casework and counseling, and the movement toward the consolidation of services and their separation from financial aid.

Among the services counted in 1969 were the following: day care, 75,900 children in 40,500 families; homemaker services, 38,300 children in 10,000 families; and foster family care, 267,000 children—largely a function of child welfare services.[26] Except for foster family care, about three-fourths of these services were provided through AFDC, a fact that suggests that AFDC services are supplanting the traditional child welfare services. Moreover, an increasing volume of child care, ranging from day care to family planning, is being purchased through the AFDC program from other agencies.

Additional child care services are provided in connection with the WIN program. Although the manpower services are responsible for the training and job placement functions, welfare agencies are responsible for child care and other services. There is considerable and justifiable criticism of the WIN program, for example, the compulsory work requirements and the poor record of training and job placement.

However, experience with WIN has served to dramatize the problems of the working mother and the need to provide adequate care for her children. Indeed, any attempt to reduce the number of dependent families with children by requiring work will have to face that reality, a fact not lost on even the strongest advocates of "workfare not welfare."

Because of the high proportion of AFDC families headed by females, a large number of WIN enrollees are mothers. Thus, as of December 1970, enrolled in WIN were 53,800 mothers with a total of 127,000 children, of whom 57,000 were under 6 years of age.[27] (Because mothers of children under 6 are not required to enroll in WIN, but may do so voluntarily, the number with preschool children is significant.) About 100,000 children were reported to have been provided with care under WIN, and the numbers are steadily increasing. However, most mothers made their own arrangements for their children; about 40 percent in their own homes, 20 percent in the homes of friends and relatives, 19 percent in family day care, 17 percent in day care centers, 1 percent in group day care, and 2 percent unknown. The questionable quality of some of these arrangements and facilities are cause for alarm.

The attempt to separate social services from financial aid has precipitated a search for new models of service delivery and new methods and approaches. One approach is a systems model in which a group of specialists, coordinated by a master programmer, brings a package of services—employment, housing, transportation, and the like—to bear on specific client problems.[28] This might be termed an "impact" model. Other models are designed to exploit the energy and creativity of young generalist workers in a loosely structured system in which advocacy is stressed.[29] In between are programs that feature decentralized neighborhood service centers, team approaches, and a "facilitative" stance, with varying degrees of professional input.

Despite the contrasts, these approaches have certain common characteristics: service is voluntary and the proportion of AFDC families "in service" at any one time is relatively small; services are focused sharply on the client's own perceived needs and generally involve "hard services"; a major part of the worker's activities are "crisis interventions" involving short-term contacts (described by one worker as "scrounging"); the emphasis on advocacy and work with groups and community organizations challenge the concept of the worker "caseload" and traditional models of social casework; and, while AFDC families still comprise the bulk of the service population, workers are reaching out beyond this group.

Only impressions from isolated studies are available, but they indicate some promising results. Service workers are freed from paperwork, clients seem to understand that services are voluntary, workers and clients tend to agree on service needs, and clients perceive the worker's attitudes and activities as generally helpful.[30]

Although official policy intends services to reduce dependency, they may possibly have the opposite outcome. First, emphasis has shifted to hard services. Day care, medical services, and even transportation are costly as compared to the counseling given during occasional home visits. So people may have earnings, but still be dependent upon the provision of the services. Second, an element of advocacy creeps in. Community participation and outreach appear to encourage an advocacy stance, especially among newer and younger workers. One worker, outposted to a migrant farm program, characterized her job as "drumming up business" for the eligibility staff. Another was placed with the community welfare council of a large city. In this capacity he was instrumental in organizing an aggressive lobby for AFDC applicants and recipients.

It is not suggested that these developments will have a

major impact on the overall AFDC caseload or its administration. They do suggest that the potential exists for the development of a viable system of social services.[31] On the other hand, those developments are hardly consistent with the stated intent of services legislation.

POLICY ISSUES

From her studies of poverty, Orshansky was led to suggest that the chief legacy poor parents have to hand on to their children is their own poverty: "Although adequate family income alone is not a sufficient condition to guarantee that children will escape low-income status as adults, it is usually a necessary one." [32] It follows that the goal of income maintenance policy should be to enable poor families to break out of poverty, not simply to alleviate it.

Schorr proposes a family life-cycle model of analysis in which poor families pass through four stages in the development of family income:

1. Timing and the circumstances of the initial marriage or child bearing.
2. Timing and direction of occupational choice.
3. Family cycle squeeze.
4. Family breakdown.[33]

The choices families make during the early stages largely determine the choices available to them at subsequent stages.

As a general rule, early marriage and parenthood mean interrupted or shortened education, a large family, and, in the long run, unemployment and underemployment. In the second stage, the young breadwinner enters the labor market already handicapped, his occupational choices and mobility seriously curtailed, and burdened with the immediate income requirements of his family. There is a good possibility that the family is already defeated. In the third stage, the family's needs accelerate and overrun income-earning capacity, which sets in motion the "family cycle squeeze" between aspiration and need, especially if the family is a large one. If the family is not successful in dealing with the squeeze, stage four, family breakdown, follows. This cycle is repeated by the children, and for the same reasons.

Seen from the perspective of this conceptual framework, AFDC provides too little, too late, under the wrong conditions. By the time a family reaches the point of seeking assistance, its future may already have been determined. Complete families have been disqualified as a matter of policy until they have exhausted their resources—in other words, until they have reached a prescribed "standard of destitution." Once on AFDC, the high tax rate precludes building up any surplus beyond survival level, the emphasis on the father's absence works against family stability, and the meager grant and unpredictable and onerous conditions under which it is given are demoralizing. If the family succeeds in leaving AFDC—or is pushed off—its situation is little better.

At best, therefore, AFDC alleviates need; it does little to provide the flexibility and choices that might enable a poor family to alter the direction in which it is moving. At worst, AFDC policies are virtually a conspiracy against poor families with children.

The civil rights movement and the war on poverty have stimulated an emphasis on the legal rights of the poor, and litigation has produced a considerable expansion of social welfare law. The thrust of these efforts has been to attempt to translate general human needs and moral rights into enforceable legal rights and to incorporate legal concepts and principles into the administration of welfare programs.

TenBroek refers to the "law of the poor" as the body of rules applicable to the poor as a distinct class and points up how their rights have been ignored or eroded by denials of due process and equal protection and by unreasonable invasions of privacy.[34] Although the "dual system of law" is a pervasive phenomenon, it is most clearly illustrated in AFDC. The different legal status of the recipient is expressed both in special liabilities connected with the receipt of assistance and in the way AFDC is administered. So widespread is the failure to comply with federal laws and with the states' own laws and regulations that Cloward was led to describe welfare administration as "lawless." [35]

Fair hearing and appeals procedures have had little effect in correcting the abuses of administrative discretion.[36] In spite of some dramatic successes, it is now clear that the judicial process has a limited capacity to control the illegalities and inequities of public assistance policy and administration. Courts cannot police bureaucracies; recipients cannot risk challenging welfare departments through litigation, nor have they the resources; and legal services are limited. The era that saw the U.S. Supreme Court take an active role in shaping public policy in this area seems to be at an end. Finally, the most important policies are made by legislatures that control appropriations and thus—with finality—programs.

Systematic disfavoring of a substantial segment of the population and widespread violation of legal rights by government reinforce apathy, frustration, and alienation among the poor. By emphasizing the preferred position of whites in the job market and under social security and unemployment compensation, it emphasizes the divisions between white and nonwhite. The social insurances require a substantial work history and do not cover low-paying or irregular kinds of employment in which nonwhites are overrepresented. Consequently, nonwhites turn to the remedial public assistance programs where they are subjected to more rigorous or offensive treatment. Such practices tend to erode values like democracy and equality and aggravate cynicism.

AFDC AND A SOCIAL POLICY FOR CHILDREN

If the AFDC program is inadequate and the consequences of its inadequacies so costly, why is the situation tolerated? To address this question it is useful to conceive of AFDC as program and AFDC as policy. That is, program can be viewed in terms of inputs—expenditures, staff, and things—whereas policy must be viewed in terms of outputs, that is, goals and outcomes. Moynihan suggests that the failure to make this distinction and to establish clearly articulated policies to guide programs has led to some very unfortunate consequences.[37]

Seen as program, the solutions to the AFDC "problem" are obvious—less restrictive eligibility requirements, higher grants, and more efficient and equitable administration. Seen as policy, however, AFDC expresses the conflicts, paradoxes, and dilemmas of public social policy regarding families with children. Consequently, the problems of AFDC can be resolved only as the United States evolves a more consistent and coherent social policy for children.

That the United States does not have such a policy is self-evident. It has a collection of more or less related programs that are internally inconsistent and in conflict with one another. The anomaly of the "absent parent" provision has been noted, although its original rationale—to restrict assistance to the unemployable, with work for the employable—could be mustered in its defense. The facts, however, no longer support that dichotomy. To pick another example, a disinterested observer of the American scene must surely wonder at the logic of a system that pays a foster parent three times as much to care for someone else's child as it pays a natural parent to care for his own child. The incongruities of the WIN program are pointed out in a report that states, "AFDC, in the great majority of states, pays the mother less to take care of her own children's needs—including food, clothing, and shelter —than it will cost to provide 'quality' day care for those same children when the mother is employed." [38]

One state, Pennsylvania, sets forth the principles and goals of protective services for children as follows:

. . . to protect the rights and welfare of children and to ensure that they have an opportunity for healthy growth and development. These rights include: adequate food, shelter, clothing, and medical care; appropriate educational, recreational, and religious opportunities; adequate adult supervision, which includes affection and guidance; and suitable protection from exposure to unwholesome and demoralizing circumstances, exploitation, and physical abuse.[39]

Taken literally, the state itself would be the worst violator of the regulations in view of its inadequate AFDC grants and the conditions in its institutions for children.

Federal and state statutes are a mélange of conflicting policies. Thus, one goal, "to maintain and strengthen family life," is potentially or actually contradictory to another, "to attain and retain capacity for self-support." In a program whose purpose is to "maintain the integrity of the family," success is measured in terms of the ability to keep the costs of assistance under control. On the other hand, by a twist of logic, proposals to deal with the "welfare crisis" would extend coverage to a much larger population, in particular to the working poor, and would vastly increase expenditures.

In discussing the confused legal status of the child, Forer notes the striking fact that neither statute nor case law establishes children's rights even to such basics as a home, education, liberty, or life itself.[40] There is, for example, no national policy that guarantees to every child a decent income, let alone medical care, education, or protection against arbitrary denial of liberty.

What might cause the United States to move toward such a social policy? Piven and Cloward advance the theory of welfare as a means of "regulating the poor," in effect, a means of regulating their labor in the interests of a capitalist economy.[41] They contend that the precipitous expansion of AFDC in the 1960s was a political response to political disorder and a greater acceptance of assistance as a right. The poor, however, are a relative minority today. It is not likely that legislators will be greatly influenced by their political power. On the other hand, unadulterated humanitarianism has never been an important factor in public social policy—for the poor in general or for any disadvantaged minority. The fiscal crisis of the states may force the federalization of AFDC—by whatever name—but this is not necessarily a fundamental departure from present policy. It might be simply a transfer of program administration—with the same policies—to another level of government.

These considerations do not bode well for poor children, those served by AFDC and the millions more who are excluded from the program. The children who do receive AFDC suffer the humiliation of the welfare stigma and the degradation of punitive policies and meager grants. Not only does the program treat them badly, but it operates to trap their families in poverty rather than to help them to escape from poverty's grasp. AFDC children are defined in law as less worthy, and the thrust of procedures and practices is to reinforce that premise. The constructive potential of social services and manpower services has been perverted by their incorporation into a program that defines their clientele as unworthy and focuses attention on the presumed shortcomings of the families instead of on the societal factors that cause poverty.

One returns, therefore, to the central theme of this discussion. AFDC is not an appropriate response to the problem of childhood poverty. What is needed is a consistent and coherent social policy for all children, a component of which would be a scheme of income guarantees that does not differentiate between poor and nonpoor children and provides the means for poor families to escape from poverty. By implication, this means a "universal" approach, one in which benefits are provided to all children without regard to their financial status. AFDC, or its equivalent, could then become what it is suited for, namely, a flexible supplementary program for particular families whose special needs and circumstances cannot be accommodated by the "universal" systems of cash and in-kind maintenance. This would make AFDC less significant in the overall picture of income maintenance for children, but no less essential.

NOTES

1. *Social Security Bulletin,* 34, no. 12 (December 1971), 54–55.
2. *Welfare in Review,* 2, no. 3 (March 1964), 16–17.
3. For a discussion of variations in local administration, see Alvin L. Schorr and Carl Wagner, *Cash and Food Programs in Virginia,* a study for the U.S. Senate Select Committee on Nutrition and Human Needs, September 23, 1969, mimeographed.
4. Social and Rehabilitation Service, *Characteristics of State Public Assistance Plans Under the Social Security Act,* 1970 ed. (Washington, D.C.: Government Printing Office, 1971).
5. George Hoshino, "Money and Morality: Income Security and Personal Social Services," *Social Work,* 16, no. 2 (April 1971), 16–24.

6. Winifred Bell, *Aid to Dependent Children* (New York: Columbia University Press, 1965), p. 175.
7. *Goldberg* v. *Kelly,* March 23, 1970, *U.S. Law Week,* 38 (March 1970), 4223–4232.
8. U.S. Bureau of the Census, *Current Population Reports,* Consumer Income, Series P-60, No. 81, "Characteristics of the Low-Income Population, 1970" (Washington, D.C.: Government Printing Office, 1971), p. 2.
9. Advisory Council on Public Welfare, *Having the Power, We Have the Duty* (Washington, D.C.: Government Printing Office, 1966), p. xii.
10. Social and Rehabilitation Service, *Findings of the 1969 AFDC Study,* pt. 2, Table 60.
11. Bureau of Social Science Research, *Welfare Policy and Its Consequences for the Recipient Population: A Study of the AFDC Program* (Washington, D.C.: Government Printing Office, 1969), pp. 24–27.
12. The President's Commission on Income Maintenance Programs, *Poverty Amid Plenty: The American Paradox* (Washington, D.C.: Government Printing Office, 1969), pp. 17–18.
13. Thomas S. Langer, Edward L. Greene, Joseph H. Henson, Jean D. Jameson, Jeanne A. Goff, John Rostkowski, and David Zykorie, "Psychiatric Impairment in Welfare and Nonwelfare Children," *Welfare in Review,* 7, no. 2 (March–April 1969), 10–21.
14. Alvin L. Schorr, *Slums and Social Insecurity* (Washington, D.C.: Government Printing Office, 1963), pp. 7–33.
15. Social and Rehabilitation Service, *Preliminary Report of Findings—1967 AFDC Study,* October 1968.
16. Elaine M. Burgess and Daniel O. Price, *An American Dependency Challenge* (Chicago: American Public Welfare Association, 1963), p. 50.
17. Bureau of Social Science Research, *Welfare Policy,* pp. 31–32.
18. Perry Levinson, "The Next Generation: A Study of Children in AFDC Families," *Welfare in Review,* 7, no. 2 (March–April 1969), 1–9.
19. Robert M. O'Neil, *The Price of Dependency* (New York: E. P. Dutton, 1970), pp. 276–280.
20. Social and Rehabilitation Service, *Preliminary Report of Findings—1967 AFDC Study,* p. 3.
21. Social and Rehabilitation Service, *Findings of the 1969 AFDC Study,* December 1970, pt. 1, Table 42.
22. Social and Rehabilitation Service, *Social Services for Families and Children,* as of December 1969, undated.

23. Joel F. Handler and Ellen Jane Hollingsworth, *The Administration of Social Services in AFDC: The Views of Welfare Recipients* (Madison, Wis.: Institute for Research on Poverty, 1969).
24. Dorothy Miller, "Effectiveness of Social Services to AFDC Recipients," Appendix I, to California State Assembly Committee on Social Welfare, *California Welfare: A Legislative Program for Reform* (Sacramento: California Legislature, 1969).
25. Governor's Task Force on Welfare Management, *Social Services in New Jersey* (Trenton, N.J., 1971), pp. 20–32.
26. Social and Rehabilitation Service, *Social Services for Families and Children*, NCSS Report E-6, December 1969.
27. Social and Rehabilitation Services, *Services to AFDC Families*, July 1971.
28. Jack C. Bloedorn, Elizabeth B. MacLatchie, William Friedlander, and J. M. Wedemeyer, *Designing Social Service Systems* (Chicago: American Public Welfare Association, 1970); also, Robert Moon and Sharon Bishop, "The APWA Model of Social Services" (paper presented to the American Public Welfare Association Northeast Regional Conference, Atlantic City, N.J., September 9, 1971).
29. Shirley Weber, "From 'Separation' to a 'Turned On' Model of Services" (paper presented to the American Public Welfare Association Northeast Regional Conference, Atlantic City, N.J., September 9, 1971).
30. Colin W. Wright, *Second Quarterly Report: Service Evaluation Program,* mimeographed (San Jose, Calif.: Santa Clara County Department of Social Welfare, 1971). Also, Gerald Fisher, field reports for doctoral dissertation, "The Separation of Social Services from Financial Aid," School of Social Work, University of Pennsylvania (in preparation).
31. Although abuses of discretion in the administration of money have been extensively documented, little attention has been paid to the potential for similar abuse with regard to services. Social services such as day care, medical care, and transportation are forms of income, and social workers may give or withhold them. Whether services can be truly voluntary under these circumstances is debatable. The low-income client is still dependent on the agency and is vulnerable to the discretionary power of the worker. See Joel Handler, "The Coercive Children's Officer," *New Society,* 12 (October 3, 1968), 485–487, and George Hoshino, "Money and Morality: Income Security and Personal Social Services," *Social Work,* 16, no. 2 (April 1971), 16–24.

32. Mollie Orshansky, "Children of the Poor," *Social Security Bulletin,* 26, no. 7 (July 1963), 12.
33. Alvin L. Schorr, *Poor Kids* (New York: Basic Books, 1966), pp. 23–48.
34. Jacobus tenBroek and the editors of *California Law Review,* eds., *The Law of the Poor* (San Francisco: Chandler Publishing Co., 1966), p. vii.
35. Richard Cloward, "A Strategy of Disruption," *Center Diary: 16,* January–February, 1967, p. 34.
36. Beatrice Vulcan, *Fair Hearings in the Public Assistance Programs of the New York City Department of Public Welfare* (Ph.D. diss., Columbia University School of Social Work, 1972), pp. 299–307.
37. Daniel P. Moynihan, "Policy vs. Program in the 70's," *Public Interest,* no. 20 (Summer 1970), 99–100.
38. Auerbach Corporation, *An Appraisal of the Work Incentive Program* (Washington: Social and Rehabilitation Service, 1970), pp. 5–6.
39. Pennsylvania Department of Public Welfare, Office of Children and Youth, *Manual,* Protective Services for Children, Section 4202, Principles and Goals.
40. Lois G. Forer, "Rights of Children: The Legal Vacuum," *American Bar Association Journal,* 55 (December 1969), 1151–1156.
41. Frances Fox Piven and Richard A. Cloward, *Regulating the Poor: The Functions of Public Welfare* (New York: Pantheon Books, 1971), pp. 320–348.

6

Health Care of Poor Children

**CHARLES U. LOWE
AND DUANE F. ALEXANDER**

A poor American child is said to be disadvantaged in the education he receives in school, the justice he receives in court, the housing in which he must live, and his lifetime opportunities. Years of delay in reading and arithmetic achievement are readily documented.[1] Despite legal services programs, accounts of unequal justice persist. But it is in health status that poor children are most strikingly disadvantaged. The clustering of morbidity and mortality in this segment of the population is stark evidence of deprivation. The federal government has become the principal provider of health services for 16 million medically indigent children in this country. We will describe this federal complex of health services and authorities, appraise its effectiveness, and compare publicly and privately supported health care.

America's children receive health care under two clearly distinguishable systems. In one, the physician is paid directly by the patient or his insurer. In the other, fees are paid from public revenues. The two systems operate in parallel, sometimes using the same professionals, but coming together almost exclusively in large teaching centers and hospitals. The private system serves the middle and upper socioeconomic classes. The public system serves 25 to 50 million poor children and adults. The federal government meets the largest share of the public cost; state and local governments also participate.

THE PUBLIC HEALTH CARE SYSTEM

The federal government became an active force in child health care in 1935. The Social Security Act provided money to states to improve the health of mothers and children and to treat crippled children. These Maternal and Child Health Programs now provide a broad range of services, including maternity and well-child clinics, school health screening, immunization, and public health nurses. As the programs have evolved, services have broadened, and emphasis has shifted from primarily rural areas to cities as well.

The migration of the rural poor to cities following World War II—at the same time that physicians were leaving the cities for the suburbs—overwhelmed the urban health care system. Convinced that inadequate obstetric care contributes to the national burden of defective and retarded children, Congress in 1963 provided for Maternity and Infant Care (M & I) Projects. These provide full maternity care and care of the infant during the first year of life. In contrast to the statewide Maternal and Child Health Programs, M & I care is usually limited to a rural county, a city, or a convenient subdivision of a city.

Spurred by testimony of children waiting in overcrowded emergency rooms because no doctor was available, Congress in 1965 authorized grants "to promote the health of children

TABLE 6-1
Federal Medical Programs for Children—Fiscal Year 1971

Program	FEDERAL BUDGET (THOUSANDS)		PEOPLE SERVED	
	Total	Child Health	Total	Children
Comprehensive Care				
Children and Youth	$ 43,800	$ 43,800	481,700	481,700 °
Maternity and Infant	38,600	N.A.	188,840	47,840 †
Health Services Development	108,813	N.A.		
(Community Health Centers)	(65,918)		260,000	130,000 °
Comprehensive Health Services	99,000	N.A.	400,000	184,000 ‡
(Neighborhood Health Centers)				
Indian Health Service	122,729	N.A.	420,000	210,000 §
Military Dependents	1,703,783	596,325	N.A.	2,216,000 °
Subtotal	$2,116,725			3,269,540
Episodic Care				
Medicaid	$3,220,142	$661,000‖	17,000,000	8,700,000 °

Component Care				
Maternal and Child Health	$ 59,250	N.A.	200,000	200,000 #
Crippled Children's Service	58,600	$ 58,600	490,000	490,000 °
Dental Care Projects	500	500	10,000	10,000
Head Start	360,000	36,000‖	472,000	472,000
Follow Through	69,000	6,900‖	60,200	60,200
Aid for Educationally Deprived Children	1,300,000	28,000	8,344,400	2,000,000‖
Migrant Health	15,062	N.A.	152,270	106,500 §
Health Services Formula Grants	90,000	N.A.	N.A.	N.A.
Subtotal	$1,952,412			3,338,700

SOURCE: Compiled from various sources, including the *Catalog of Federal Domestic Assistance*, records of House and Senate Appropriations Committee hearings, publications of the government agencies involved, and personal communications from officials of these agencies.

N.A. = Not Available

° Under 21 years of age.

† Under 1 year of age.

‡ Under 15 years of age.

§ Under 17 years of age.

‖ Estimated.

This figure represents children receiving general pediatric clinic service from MCHS. Special clinic services range from mental retardation clinics serving 45,000 to vision screening serving 10,000,000.

and youth of school and preschool age, particularly in areas with concentrations of low-income families." The Children and Youth (C & Y) Projects, many of them operated by medical schools, provide comprehensive medical care to children in prescribed areas. By 1971, projects to provide dental care were added as a separate program.

With the poverty program, the government undertook new experiments in health delivery and, in particular, financed a number of comprehensive Neighborhood Health Centers. Partnership for Health, enacted in 1966, has met special health needs (rubella immunization, tuberculosis case finding, and so on) and has also supported comprehensive family health centers in disadvantaged communities. Three educational initiatives of the 1960s—Head Start, Follow Through, and the Elementary and Secondary Education Act—provide health services to children as an expression of the view that education and health are related. Finally, there are a variety of special programs—for children of migrant laborers, for Indians, and for children with birth defects, mental retardation, and emotional illness.

All the foregoing programs, though they make an impressive listing, reach perhaps a million children a year with comprehensive care and perhaps a million more with special services (exclusive of screening). The really consequential federal program is Medicaid. Medicaid pays for acute medical care for the so-called medically needy. Federal payments are based primarily on what states are themselves willing to spend; consequently the bulk of federal money goes to the wealthier states. Thus, New York receives more per recipient than Mississippi.

Other programs rely on Medicaid for part of their financing. For example, 31 percent of the costs of Community Health Centers comes from patient fees provided by Medicaid or private insurers. Most of Medicaid's cost is for acute or chronic illness rather than for comprehensive or preventive care.

Table 6–1 lists the federal programs that provide health care for children, with their costs and estimated patient loads.

IMPACT OF FEDERAL HEALTH PROGRAMS

The impact of this wide variety of federal health programs is difficult to assess; we may begin with an examination of health indices compiled before most of these recently initiated programs could be expected to have a demonstrable effect (see Table 6–2). National health statistics are frequently not tabulated according to economic status of the population; for purposes of analysis we may infer the status of those who are poor from the status of blacks. As some blacks have high incomes and some whites have low incomes, such an approximation tends, if anything, to understate the differences between poor and nonpoor.

Infant mortality rate has been called the best social indicator of child health. In 1970, the infant mortality rate per thousand live births was 17.4 for whites and 31.4 for nonwhites.[2] In 1966, the most recent year for which such data are available, the rate in families with incomes above $7,000 per year was 19.6, while it was 31.8 in families with incomes under $3,000.[3] Sharper contrasts may be cited. For example, in New York City in 1967, the infant mortality rate was 13.0 in the well-to-do district of Maspeth-Forest Hills and 41.5 in central Harlem.[4]

A child born to a poor family is more likely to be born prematurely. For instance, in 1968 the prematurity rate was 7.1 percent for whites and 13.7 percent for nonwhites.[5] (As a con-

TABLE 6-2

Health Status and Medical Care
(Selected Indices for the United States)

	Year	Total	White	Non-white	Non-poor	Poor
Health Status Indicators						
1. Infant mortality [2]	1970	19.8	17.4	31.4	—	—
(deaths / 1000 live births) [3]	1966	23.7	20.6	38.8	19.6	31.8
2. Life expectancy (years) [6]	1968	70.2	71.1	63.7	—	—
3. Prematurity rate (%) [5]	1968	8.2	7.1	13.7	—	—
4. Duration of hospital stay (average no. of days) [12]	1968	6.3	5.6	11.3	5.1	10.2
5. Children under 15 hospitalized per year (%) [12]	1968	5.08	5.3	3.9	4.74	5.23
6. Average bed disability days per year (children under 17) [10]	1967	4.3	4.4	3.7	4.1	5.1
7. Average no. of school days lost per year [9]	1968	5.0	4.9	5.2	4.8	5.5
8. Average restricted activity-days per year (adults over 25) [11]	1968	19.8	19.0	26.8	14.6	33.4
Medical Care Indicators						
1. Physician seen during year (%) [7]	1967	68.0	70.8	52.5	74.0	52.9
2. Average no. of physician visits per year [8]	1969	3.7	3.9	2.5	3.9	2.8
3. Average no. of dental visits per year [13]	1968	1.2	—	—	1.4	0.4
4. Children (under 17) never seeing dentist (%) [14]	1964	42.6	38.7	66.1	27.3	61.7
5. Average no. of teeth filled/decayed [16]	1965	—	—	—	3.6/0.7	0.7/3.4

SOURCE: Superior numbers in this table refer to the notes for Chapter 6, see pages 159–161.

sequence of prematurity, infants have increased risk of mental retardation; the prevalence of mental subnormality among the poor is many times as high as it is among the nonpoor.) Life expectancy at birth, a number that reflects infant mortality plus lifelong health care, shows a similar differential. White infants born in the United States in 1968 had an average life expectancy of 71.1 years, compared to 63.7 years for nonwhites.[6]

Poor children also receive less medical care and suffer more disability than other children. In 1967, 53% of children in families with income under $3,000 per year saw a physician, compared to 74% in families with incomes over $7,000.[7] In 1969 children in poor families averaged 2.8 physician visits per year as against 3.9 visits by children in higher-income families.[8] The directly measurable effect on morbidity of receiving less medical care may be slight. For example, in 1968 children in families with incomes below $5,000 lost 5.5 days from school, and children in families earning above $5,000 lost 4.8 days.[9] Similarly, children in low-income (below $3,-000) families spent 5.1 days in bed, disabled, in 1967 compared to 4.1 days for children in families with incomes above $7,000.[10]

The chronic toll is higher. In 1968, adults with incomes below $5,000 reported 33.4 days of restricted activity, compared to 14.6 days for those with incomes above $5,000.[11] While there is a modest difference in the percentage of poor and nonpoor children hospitalized each year (5.23 percent and 4.74 percent, respectively), children in families with incomes below $3,000 stay in the hospital twice as long as those in families earning over $10,000 (10.2 versus 5.1 days).[12] The longer stay probably reflects more severe illness and more difficulty in meeting medical needs at home among poor families.

Data on dental disease and care shows similar trends. Children in families with incomes below $3,000 paid an average of 0.4 dental visits in 1968, while those with family incomes above $7,000 averaged 1.4 visits.[13] In 1964, 62 percent of poor children had never seen a dentist, compared with 27 percent in families earning $7,000.[14] It was estimated in 1969 that 23 million children had never seen a dentist.[15] In 1965, of children aged 6 to 11 years, those in families with incomes under $3,000 averaged 0.7 filled and 3.4 decayed teeth, while those in families with incomes over $15,000 averaged 3.6 filled and 0.7 decayed teeth.[16] The conclusion is obvious. Tooth decay strikes both groups alike, but the poor do not receive dental care.

Apart from national surveys, other sources document inadequate health care among poor children. Initial findings from Head Start in 1965 showed that 20 to 40 percent of the children had iron deficiency anemia.[17] Tooth decay was found in 40 to 90 percent of the children, depending on whether their water supply was fluoridated. One-third had not been seen by a physician in over two years, and 75 percent had never seen a dentist. Half had not been fully immunized. Similarly, government studies document that in two out of five cases of assistance to dependent children, dental care was needed, but not provided; the same was true of eyeglasses in one out of three cases, and of medical care in one out of four cases.[18] More recent surveys show the same picture. For example, 1,178 Mississippi children on Medicaid in 1970 had 1,301 abnormal conditions—tooth decay, anemia, poor vision, cardiac anomalies, parasites, hernias, and so forth.[19]

In short, poor children see the doctor and dentist less, stay longer in the hospital when they get there, suffer from a variety of untreated and undiagnosed illnesses, are disabled more often during their lifetime, and do not live as long in the end. Is this because they are not reached by health programs, or because they receive inadequate care when they are reached? Answering the first question requires an estimate of the number of children reached by the private and public systems, an estimate that can be arrived at only by indirect calculation.

In 1970, about 10,500 pediatricians were engaged in full-time private practice. An additional 52,000 general practitioners spent one-fourth of their time, on the average, caring for children; in time spent, they were equivalent to 13,000 pediatricians. Physicians average 7,600 patient visits a year [20] and each child is seen 3.6 times,[21] on the average. Thus, we conclude that physicians in private practice cared for an average of 2,100 children each, or 49.3 million children all told.

Children served by the public system in 1971 totaled no more than 15.3 million (see Table 6–1). Most of these children participated in Medicaid (8.7 million) or received certain special services only (3.3 million) and were purchasing care largely from the private system. Only 3.3 million children were receiving care totally from the public system. Adding these to our estimate of 49.3 million children receiving care from private physicians reveals that a total of 52.6 million children received care in 1971. But there were 62.7 million children under 16 years of age; 10 million children apparently received no health care at all! (An unknown number of children received some form of health care from physicians in institutions—university hospitals, primarily. Some are counted among the 15.3 million served by the public system, but the exact number is unavailable.)

Lack of care for poor children may be only part of the problem. We do not know how many children were treated for an acute illness, without regard for follow-up or other existing conditions. How many children moved back and forth between the two systems, receiving cursory care from both? These groups of children that fall between the loose weave formed by both systems and receive no care or poor care may be the major shortcoming of the dual system.

Thus, some children are truly not reached by health care programs. No wonder nearly half of poor children are reported as having seen no physician all year. What may be said about the second question—whether the children who are seen are adequately served? In an attempt to answer, we turn again to an evaluation of vital statistics. In 1971, the Maternal and Child Health Service reported the following facts as evidence of the beneficial impact of its services.[22]

1. In the seven years before initiation of M & I Projects in 1964, the infant mortality rate in the United States fell only from 26.0 to 25.2 per thousand; in the seven years after, the rate fell from 25.2 to 19.8. For nonwhites the comparable rates were 43.7 to 41.5 and 41.5 to 31.4 respectively.
2. In the lowest socioeconomic census tracts in Denver, Colorado, served by the M & I Project, the infant mortality rate dropped from 34.2 in 1964 to 21.5 in 1969.
3. In Richmond, Virginia, in 1969, the infant mortality rate for M & I Project patients was 16.5 compared to the city rate of 26.4.
4. In St. Louis, Missouri, the infant mortality rate in the M & I Project fell from 44.4 in 1965 to 31.1 in 1970.
5. Children registered in the C & Y Projects have experienced a 50 percent decrease in hospital admissions since the program was initiated, a factor which partially accounts for a decrease in cost of care per child from $201.26 in 1968 to $149.82 in 1970. In addition, diagnosis of "well child" on recall examination has increased over 50 percent.

Statistics cited by the Indian Health Service in 1971 show that since the Public Health Service assumed responsibility for Indian health in 1955, the infant mortality rate among Indians had declined 51 percent, and babies born in hospitals have increased from 88.2 percent to 98.0 percent.[23]

These figures suggest that the programs have a beneficial impact and that children receive health care of good quality. On the other hand, not all these programs have had comparable impact. For instance, the infant mortality rate in Baltimore declined only from 26.8 to 25.1 between 1965 and 1970 despite an active M & I Project.[24] Systematic evidence is wholly lacking concerning the quality of government care. One has to conduct a search for such evidence to accept the astonishing fact that there is literally no reporting or evaluation of the quality of medical care for poor children, or, in fact, for children using the private system.

One cogent observation about quality can be made: No more than a million medically indigent children receive public medical care that is comprehensive in nature. In theory, states are required to screen children in Medicaid-eligible families and provide the treatment they need. In fact, as of March 1972 only five states had complied with even the screening requirement. So the large number of poor children are receiving care only for acute illnesses or certain specially selected components (immunization, and so on), if they receive care at all. They are not receiving comprehensive or preventive care. On that score alone, the answer to the question whether children are suffering from poor medical care has to be yes.

It may be said, in summary, that the public system is deficient and that its deficiencies differ from those of the private system. It has been apparent for a number of years that neither system meets the goal of providing optimal health care. The private health system is expensive, inefficient, and unevenly distributed, but it is capable of delivering superb care to those who can find and pay for it. Patients commonly relate to a single physician, though they may benefit from consultation and may use specialists. Those who cannot pay for the private system use the public system. This system costs the patient little, is largely limited to city residents, is oriented to the convenience of the physician and health professional rather than the patient, and usually supplies only episodic or emergency care. Certainly high-quality care is possible, but in actual practice service is far too often fragmented, is supplied by many different professionals to the same patient, is frequently impersonal, and is at times ineffective or even inappropriate.

COSTS OF THE TWO SYSTEMS

The costs of the public and private medical care systems show little difference. In 1970, the total cost of personal health care in the United States was $58 billion. Only $9.3 billion (16 percent) was for care of children under 19 years of age—a per capita expenditure of $123. Distribution of the per capita cost showed that $33 was for hospital care, $41 for physicians' services, and $49 for other health services. Private funds provided 73 percent and public funds 27 percent of this total.[25] The American Academy of Pediatrics estimates that the annual cost per child for private health care is $110 to $130.[26] In 1971 the federal government spent $1.672 billion to provide health care to approximately 15.3 million children, or $110 per child.[27] Of this amount $838 million was spent for indigent children. This per capita cost is an underestimate, because matching funds are added to many programs and because some children covered by Medicaid may be counted twice.

More accurate per capita costs can be calculated for two specific federal programs. The cost of providing complete medical care for 2.216 million dependent children of military personnel in 1971 was $596 million, a per capita cost of $269.[28] In the C & Y Projects, comprehensive medical and dental care was provided to 434,300 children in 1971 at a total (federal and matching) cost of $60.9 million, or $140.22 per child per year.

With the exception of the military program, the estimates converge to make $130 per child appear as a common and acceptable cost of health care for children. Dr. Helen Wallace has pointed out that *comprehensive* health care, along the lines of C & Y clinics and at current program costs, could be provided for all children for little more than is already being spent.[29] The cost—$10.5 billion—would be only about $1 billion more than expenditures from all sources for child health care in 1970. Alternatively, if comprehensive care comparable to C & Y Projects were substituted for the dozen or more partial and special federal programs now in existence, *all* 16 million medically indigent children could receive care for $2 billion, little more than was spent by the federal government in 1971 for all its child health programs. It is hardly necessary to point out that such care would be preventive, comprehensive rather than episodic, and would include many children who now receive no care at all.

CONCLUSION

We see a picture of two systems of health care, neither operating efficiently and both together failing to serve all the children who need health services. Poor children receive less health service in all ways and show a dramatic incidence of deficiencies or illnesses.

We cannot conclude that proper and adequate health service alone would eliminate their disabilities. The poor are often ill-housed, poorly educated, malnourished, are unemployed or underemployed, and are more than ordinarily likely to be members of broken families. Good health reflects public health measures far more directly than it reflects the intervention of physicians. It can quite forcefully be argued that until the other adverse environmental factors are ameliorated, we can expect little improvement in health status of the poor.[30] Nevertheless, out of simple social justice, if not out of the expectation of striking consequences, poor children ought to be at least as well served medically as other children.

Government has become the great provider of publicly supported health service for those who cannot buy private care. So far, the public system reflects the faltering steps of a lurching giant. Society knows the dimensions and specifications of optimal health care, but has hesitated to make the public system cohesive, fiscally sound, and properly responsive to the needs of the patient. Society has been reluctant to put the public system into competition with the private one and has sustained a curious mythology about the sanctity of the medical profession. Nevertheless, there is change in the air. The public system is increasingly filling the unmet needs of the nation.

The future pattern of child health care, like that of American medicine in general, is uncertain. A number of factors indicate that the 1970s will be augural years. The requirements for periodic medical screening and treatment of Medicaid-eligible children should lead to questions about a desirable system of providing health care for children. Legislative authorization for several existing child health care programs will be expiring and will be subject to modification. Proposals to shift funding for many of these categorical programs to a revenue sharing system will, if enacted, have impact of uncertain dimensions. During 1972 and 1973 these programs struggled for survival with an uncertain budget and future. If replaced by revenue sharing or, ultimately, by some form of federally mandated health insurance, the real danger is that such programs will be episodic rather than comprehensive or preventative medicine.

In 1971 the American Academy of Pediatrics published results of a three-year study of the delivery of health care to children. The report, *Lengthening Shadows,* documents the enormous advances made over the past 20 years in our ability to keep children healthy. It identifies the gaps in the system and demonstrates that large segments of the population do not share in the benefits of advancing scientific knowledge. The academy makes 20 major recommendations for improvements in the child health delivery system. Examination of those recommendations in light of the present review forces attention to two cardinal needs.

Coordination and expansion of government health activities are probably the greatest national needs insofar as health care for poor children is concerned. As Table 6–1 shows, comprehensive care for children is now provided under six separate programs; episodic care under one; and component care through eight distinct activities. Some programs operate within the same agency; others are unique in an agency with no basic commitment to health care (Office of Economic Opportunity or the Office of Education). Each program competes for budget, personnel, and lobby; each maintains a separate staff, review system, and operating procedure. These programs (excluding that for military dependents) in theory serve but one principal client, the poor child in America. We observe a patchwork of programs, none comprehensive or omnibus in nature, yet each fulfilling an easily documented need. A necessary first step is rationalization of the government system that supplies health care service for children who are unable to purchase it privately.

There would be a gain in efficiency, but more important would be gains in simplification and flexibility. Presumably the system might then capture 10 million children who now apparently receive no health care. It remains to be seen whether these medical "dropouts" fail to receive health care only by virtue of indigence. Perhaps some live too far from physicians and hospitals, while others are victims of ignorance or parental indolence. But they apparently are not being cared for through private medicine; as in other matters, we turn to the federal government.

While national attention focuses on the defects and benefits of the public system, it must be clear that both the public and the private systems require modification, expansion, and better distribution. A simple expansion of the existing public programs will not meet the national need. For one thing, there is danger that a public program limited to those who are indigent may provide care that is inferior to that in the private system. Because it appears inevitable that we will support a dual system for the foreseeable future, a national health program insuring quality care for all children must facilitate interplay between both systems. It should use the strengths of each, encouraging optimal interaction while demanding a single standard of excellence.

What is the prospect? Powerful forces are operating to initiate change and improvement. The public is increasingly demanding health care as a right. The younger generation is insisting that we ameliorate social and economic inequality and ill-health. Health professionals have become involved in self-inspection, and some are questioning the apparent limits of a health care system built upon entrepreneurship. The entry of government into health planning has forced a more open review of available options and has given the consumer participatory rather than mendicant status. And persuasive evidence is accumulating that good health care not only reduces morbidity, but is also cheaper.

Yet, what society may recognize as essential for adults may be optional for children. It is not at all clear that the impact of illness in children is recognized with the same force as disability of a breadwinner. We cannot be certain that due consideration will be given to the needs of children as we reweave the fabric of national health care. Moreover, we think of our own children in one way and children of others in another. Although we may accept a national health program to insure the health of the wage earner, it remains to be seen whether we will do the same for children. In a society that no longer assigns an economic value to children, there may be decreasing interest in committing national resources to their care. That much is at issue.

NOTES

1. *School Achievement of Children by Demographic and Socio-economic Factors*, U.S. Department of Health, Education and Welfare, Public Health Service, Health Services and Mental Health Administration, National Center for Health Statistics, publication no. 72–1011 (Washington, D.C.: Government Printing Office, 1971), p. 15.
2. Personal communication from Lillian Freedman, Program Statistics and Analysis Branch, National Institute of Child Health and Development, National Institutes of Health.
3. *The Health of Children—1970*, U.S. Department of Health, Education, and Welfare, Public Health Service, publication no. 2121 (Washington, D.C.: Government Printing Office, 1970), p. 5.
4. *Profiles of Children*, 1970 White House Conference on Children (Washington, D.C.: Government Printing Office, 1970), p. 94.
5. *Vital Statistics of the United States, 1968*, vol. 1, U.S. Department of Health, Education, and Welfare, Public Health Service, Health Services and Mental Health Administration, National Center for Health Statistics, publication no. 0–416–832 (Washington, D.C.: Government Printing Office, 1971), pp. 1–25.
6. *Vital Statistics of the United States, 1968*, vol. 2, sec. 5, U.S. Department of Health, Education, and Welfare, Public Health Service, Health Services and Mental Health Administration, National Center for Health Statistics, publication no. 0–421–346 (Washington, D.C.: Government Printing Office, 1971), pp. 5–12.
7. *Health of Children—1970*, p. 34.
8. *Physician Visits: Volume and Interval Since Last Visit, United States—1969*, U.S. Department of Health, Education, and Welfare, Public Health Service, publication no. 72–1064, ser. 10, no. 75 (Washington, D.C.: Government Printing Office, 1972), p. 21.

9. *Children and Youth: Selected Health Characteristics*, U.S. Department of Health, Education, and Welfare, Public Health Service, publication no. 1000, ser. 10, no. 62 (Washington, D.C.: Government Printing Office, 1971), p. 25.

10. *Health of Children—1970*, p. 29.

11. *Children and Youth*, p. 24.

12. *Health of Children—1970*, p. 31.

13. *Health of Children—1970*, p. 36.

14. *Health of Children—1970*, p. 37.

15. *Current Estimates from the Health Interview Survey, United States—1969*, U.S. Department of Health, Education, and Welfare, Public Health Service, publication no. 1000, ser. 10, no. 63 (Washington, D.C.: Government Printing Office, 1971), p. 22.

16. *Health of Children—1970*, p. 37.

17. A. F. North, "Project Head Start and the Pediatrician," *Clinical Pediatrics* 6 (1967), 191–194.

18. National Center for Social Statistics, U.S. Department of Health, Education, and Welfare, 1969. 1967 AFDC Study, Table VI, "Medical Care Deprivation."

19. *Washington Post,* October 24, 1971.

20. *Reference Data on the Profile of Medical Practice, 1971* (Chicago: American Medical Association, 1971), p. 54.

21. *Health of Children—1970*, p. 35.

22. *Promoting the Health of Mothers and Children, FY 1971*, U.S. Department of Health, Education, and Welfare, Public Health Service, publication no. 72–5002 (Washington, D.C.: Government Printing Office, 1971).

23. *Indian Health Program, 1955–1971*, U.S. Department of Health, Education, and Welfare, Public Health Service, publication no. 1394 (Washington, D.C.: Government Printing Office, 1971).

24. *Promoting the Health of Mothers and Children, FY 1971.*

25. D. Rice and M. McGee, "Medical Care Outlays for Three Age Groups: Young, Intermediate, and Aged," *Social Security Bulletin*, 34, no. 5 (May 1971), 3–14.

26. Personal communication from Robert Frazier, American Academy of Pediatrics.

27. *Special Analyses, Budget of the U.S. Government, FY 1973*, Executive Office of the President, Office of Management and Budget (Washington, D.C.: Government Printing Office, 1972), p. 169.

28. *Special Analyses, Budget of the U.S. Government, FY 1971*, Executive Office of the President, Office of Management and

Budget (Washington, D.C.: Government Printing Office, 1970), p. 161.

29. H. Wallace, "Some Thoughts on Planning Health Care for Children and Youth," *Children,* 18, no. 3 (May–June 1971), 95–100.

30. R. A. Stallones, "Community Health," *Science* 175 (February 25, 1972), 839.

7

Wards of Court: A Perspective on Justice for Children

MARGARET K. ROSENHEIM

Nearly three-quarters of a century ago, experiments with, and pleas for, broad-scale measures of child welfare were capped by legislation, in Illinois, creating juvenile courts. This fateful step, as it transpired, was a popular one. All over the nation, reformers hastened to emulate the example: first, a specialized court for children, and then the accoutrements of juvenile justice—probation, diagnostic facilities, separate detention quarters, and ultimately (in many big cities) juvenile police.[1]

Today, both the rationale and practice of these juvenile courts are being questioned. The presumption of prescience and helpfulness on the part of juvenile court judges has weakened—or even toppled. Whereas the invocation of the concept of *parens patriae* formerly served to still the small voices of dissent, today some advocates of children's interests cavil at the naiveté and pretension of this concept.

This state of affairs particularly concerns juvenile specialists and is not without interest to criminologists in general.

The child welfare or child development specialist is typically less knowledgeable about this area of law and public administration. Yet, to understand the current state of child welfare, it is important to heed developments in juvenile justice. The legal status of minority (nonadulthood) is both mirror and mold of social attitudes toward children and youth. They have consequences for a large array of institutions not often thought of in terms of law. If we accept what seems plain, though hard to document—that children from low-income families dominate the juvenile justice system—study of the system illuminates the state of child welfare for this group of children.

JUVENILE COURT JURISDICTION

Juvenile justice is ordinarily described in terms of juvenile court legislation. In some places the term "family court" is used and it usually indicates a broader jurisdiction over subject matter than characterizes a juvenile court. These special courts have jurisdiction over criminal behavior, or acts that would be criminal if committed by adults. This misconduct is at the core of jurisdiction over *delinquency*. Delinquency once included conduct proscribed exclusively for children (like truancy and running away), but gradually states have distinguished noncriminal misbehavior from criminal delinquency and have encouraged nonjudicial treatment of the former. Not all states have changed, but professional and scholarly opinion clearly favors a narrow definition of delinquency. (And this is the meaning attached to the word throughout this chapter.)

Juvenile court jurisdiction has a less familiar side, too. There is authority over children at the risk, or at the mercy, of parental indifference or cruelty; this is *neglect*. There is jurisdiction over children who, through no fault of their parents, lack effective direction and care; this is *dependency*. Finally, there is jurisdiction over children who have misbehaved, but not violated a law. For example, the runaway or truant or "incorrigible" who might once have been defined delinquent is named a "person (or minor or child) in need of supervision"—in the shorthand of experts, PINS, MINS or CHINS.

Thus, there are four well-accepted classes of children—the delinquent, neglected, dependent and increasingly popular "in need of supervision." Many states give juvenile courts responsibility for an even wider range of misconduct or pathology. They may be charged with hearing cases on termination of parental rights, adoption, determination of paternity, commitment of mentally retarded children, and so forth. Where there are family courts, matters such as nonsupport and marital disputes are apt to be included. Although the types of cases vary widely from state to state, and the numbers are relatively insignificant compared to the standard business of juvenile justice, this "add-on" tendency is important. It illustrates the reliance upon courts as the ultimate treater or disciplinarian.[2] As a result, the court is a potent influence even when it appears to be remote from the immediate problems affecting a juvenile.

THE IDEA OF JUVENILE JUSTICE

To understand the present situation we need to go back briefly to the origin of juvenile courts. As Morris and Hawkins tell us:

The juvenile court emerged from what was a legal misinterpretation of the *parens patriae* concept. This concept was developed for quite different purposes—property and wardship—and had nothing to do with what juvenile courts do now. Though we keep on prating *parens patriae,* we might as well burn incense. Historical idiosyncrasies gave us a doubtful assumption of power over children. With the quasi-legal concept of *parens patriae* to brace it, this assumption of power blended well with the earlier humanitarian traditions in the churches and other charitable organizations regarding child care and child-saving. The juvenile court is thus the product of paternal error and maternal generosity, which is a not unusual genesis of illegitimacy.[3]

A concept intended to protect incompetents was transplanted to delinquency control. It fostered assumption of power over children who are themselves in danger. Indeed this bond between the quite diverse spheres of the juvenile court has been its most prominent feature. "The child savers . . . adhered to this critical philosophical position: no formal legal or juridical distinctions should be made between the delinquent child and the dependent or neglected child; they are a unity, a commonality, to be handled by a single instrumentality."[4] Crime control and child saving were wedded.

It is not hard to see why this occurred. In the young, the line between maltreatment and malfeasance is obscure. Rescue of impressionable children from unwholesome influences readily became the focus of child-saving activities. The child care specialist of the 1890s was not so much interested in what had happened—what the child did—as in what should be done. Reformers of that time were developing institutions to alter the social setting—to repair deficiencies in parental instruction, to replace the enticements of city street companions with a wholesome, often country-based, regimen, to supplant gaming and smoking and swearing with broom making, farming, and drill in the three R's.

By 1899, a host of ideas had taken concrete shape in the

form of orphanages, houses of correction, and programs of child placement, like the famous New York Children's Aid Society. A tentative step toward a liaison between rescue organizations and the courts was taken when protective societies were established in 1875. They offered "organized protection for the dependent children" and "provision of an official character for the prosecution of parents or others who ill-used and brutally treated the young and defenseless." [5] But it remained to assign public responsibility for child saving and to invent the necessary machinery. This was to be the contribution of the juvenile court.

Thus, from the outset the child welfare and crime-control functions of the juvenile court have been intertwined. Civic attention was on children who did not have what their self-appointed spokesmen thought they needed, and this lack often appeared to result from poverty. The "bad" boys and girls were in trouble because of parental incapacity or indifference; their parents were poor and often foreign born. "Good" children were classed as neglected or dependent; their parents, too, lacked education or funds.

By contrast, the children of civic leaders appeared not to require child-rescue services. The reformers' offspring attended school, did not work in factories, and gravitated to the countryside for sport and recreation. To judge by contemporary comment, they did not inhabit the houses of correction or walk the corridors of the precinct station or court.[6] Thus, it was mainly the children of the poor who furnished the juvenile court a clientele. Yet reformers and officials overlooked the connection between poverty and recourse to court. Neither questions of the proper use of state power nor sociological studies of deviancy muddied the vision of the child savers.

For all the recent attention to the deprivation that pervades the lives of juvenile justice "customers," it would be unwise to ignore the influence of juvenile court laws on all minors regardless of economic standing. The court looms in the background as the ultimate coercive authority, enforcing standards for conduct. We cannot measure how many children regularly attend school, abandon plans to run away, or contain their impulses to mayhem, owing to their subliminal appreciation of legal authority. Yet laws respecting juveniles may be presumed to have a powerful hold in that literally all juvenile behavior is controllable by some adult who can, if necessary, have recourse to court.

We have so far seen that crime control and child saving were wedded in the jurisdiction of juvenile courts and that a reformist atmosphere led, in practice, if not in philosophy, to a preoccupation with poor children in these courts. Nevertheless, the courts stand in the background to support all parental authority. Let us look now at the ambiguity that surrounds the very status of being a minor.

Certain laws about minors authorize provision of care to the young and helpless; others reflect the conviction that children are not fully responsible for their acts. The need for protective measures is beyond debate. It is the manner of their application that creates contention and uncertainty. And there are debatable points of principle.

There is, for instance, no litmus test that separates the helpless child being protected from the misguided child being constrained. Officials are strongly tempted to argue a child's vulnerability to justify a plan that enforces approved standards of juvenile deportment. "Too often what happens," comment Morris and Hawkins, "is that the rescue operations ignore the preferences of those who are to be rescued." [7] The presumption of innocence, a cardinal principle of criminal justice, gives way in juvenile courts to a presumption of loss of innocence. All court acts are asserted to be benevolent and rehabilitative, but these acts may be perceived by the child as punitive. Moreover, this rhetoric of benevolence obscures the fact that authority must often be exercised to protect the public and not exclusively, or even primarily, to protect the child.[8]

This failure to sort out the purposes served by assigning children special legal status has important consequences. It is not sufficient for the reform of juvenile justice or redirection of child welfare to break the unity that binds delinquent and dependent and neglected children together. It is also necessary to reconsider the case for special treatment of minors— the fundamental grounds, the age limits, and the procedures and sanctions.

So long as juvenile court jurisdiction comprehends all malefactions and causes of vulnerability, it is hard to imagine the child who is not subject to the court's jurisdiction. Law-violative behavior: that is a broad sweep, and recent studies confirm that there is a little criminal in each of us that finds expression as part of growing up. Neglect: an ill-defined term, sufficiently malleable to cover criminal conduct of the very young on the rationale that it arises from poor parental guidance. And "children in need of supervision": so general and imprecise as to comprehend any child during a protracted period of defiance. It should be clear that there are few limitations on juvenile court jurisdiction. More children do not come to court only because of the judgment, disinclinations, tolerance, inhibitions, or alternative resources of adults who possess the power to "make the case official."

THREE FEATURES OF JUVENILE JUSTICE

Whatever the principles of a comprehensive juvenile court and however confused its objectives, how does it work in practice? Quite specifically, what has stimulated the criticisms that have endured these past 20 years?

Juvenile courts were hailed in the beginning because of nonadversarial procedures. An informal proceeding replaced the contentious trial of questions of guilt. Petitions replaced indictments; rules of evidence gave way to experts' reports; narrowly drawn grounds for intervention were supplanted by recital of the child's need; and the fatherly judge and concerned probation officers replaced the conventional actors in the drama of litigation.

The change of roles was of great importance. On this, Jane Addams had the following to say:

Perhaps the most striking result of the Juvenile Court was that brought about in the law court as such, where lawyers have for many years ranged themselves to prosecute and to defend a prisoner. There was almost a change in *mores* when the Juvenile Court was established. The child was brought before the judge with no one to prosecute him and none to defend him—the judge and all concerned were merely trying to find out what could be done on his behalf. The element of conflict was absolutely eliminated and with it, all notion of punishment as such with its curiously belated connotation.[9]

Now, critics have zeroed in on the role of counsel as central to their attacks on the absence of procedural due process in juvenile justice.

Consider, for example, the forceful language of the President's Crime Commission:

The Commission believes that no single action holds more potential for achieving procedural justice for the child in the juvenile court than the provision of counsel. . . . The rights to confront one's accusers, to cross-examine witnesses, to present evidence and testimony of one's own, to be unaffected by prejudicial and unreliable evidence, to participate meaningfully in the dispositional decision, to take an appeal, have substantial meaning for the overwhelming majority of persons brought before the juvenile court only if they are provided with competent lawyers who can invoke those rights effectively.[10]

This illustrates a growing disenchantment with the procedural "irregularity" of juvenile courts. Partly, it ties into a broader concern about the rights and privacy of citizens and about the impact of the "therapeutic state" upon those who live at the margins of poverty.[11] But the sweeping purposes of juvenile justice, and the vulnerability of its subjects, reinforce our unease about the potential for arbitrariness in informal proceedings. The contribution of counsel lies not only in the actions they deflect or block, through the application of a healthy skepticism to assertions of benevolent purpose, but in the total climate their regular appearance will create. "Quite apart from the consequences in individual cases, it is believed that the political consequences of this new interest in a heretofore hidden social process will be of great importance." [12]

Caselaw reflects a progression from challenges to *informal* procedures, to challenges of the premises that underlie them. Attention is no longer focused on the justice of individual outcome, important as it is; it also runs to reshaping the original principles of juvenile justice. The scope of juvenile court jurisdiction is being challenged; the soundness of detention policy and denial of bail is questioned; the differences between the conditions of release and supervision in juvenile justice and in adult probation or parole are queried. And, in all likelihood, this is but the beginning of a quest for defensible distinctions between the premises and procedures of criminal law and the juvenile court system.

Two other features of juvenile justice are evident at every juncture. They are discretionary authority and a considerable overload of cases. Overload has a number of damaging consequences. As the President's Commission on Law Enforcement noted, "judicial hearings often turn out to be little more than attenuated interviews of 10 to 15 minutes duration." The commission noted further that the waiting lists [of clinical services] are so long that their usefulness is more theoretical than real. . . . A large percentage of juvenile courts have no probation service at all, and in those that do, caseloads are typically so high that counseling and supervision take the form of occasional phone calls and perfunctory visits instead of the careful, individualized service that was intended. Institutionalization too often means storage—isolation from the outside world —in an overcrowded, understaffed security institution. . . .[13]

The burden of numbers leads to other unfortunate results. Consider, for example, the average length of stay in one state training school: "In most cases it is either too long or too short. How is the norm of four and a half months reached in that institution? Simple enough: you have to find beds for the intake, so you must get rid of some at the other end." [14]

A similar principle probably operates in regulating the flow of cases from police to court, from court intake to formal petition stage, and so on. The excessive demands upon this system are particularly worrisome, given the promise of juvenile justice: that legal principles of criminal law will be replaced, for juveniles, by an informal but sensitive and individualized inquiry into the child's needs. Neither the adjudicative process nor the dispositional phase provide much ground for reassurance. In the now famous words of Mr. Justice Fortas:

There is evidence, in fact, that there may be grounds for concern that the child receives the worst of both worlds: that he gets neither the protections accorded to adults nor the solicitous care and regenerative treatment postulated for children.[15]

Beyond this, juvenile justice is riddled with discretionary authority. The infusion of social control systems—by definition authoritative and nonconsensual—with discretionary judgment broadens official opportunities for screening cases out and screening them in.[16] However much flexibility and "doing-good" this permits, it increases the possibilities for abuse of power—for overkill, for arbitrary action, and for preachment to, and humiliation of youths.

Despite inherent dangers, every juvenile justice system relies on discretion. Blanket application of the law would be too severe in numerous cases, especially as legislatures tend to "overcriminalize" conduct. And discretion plays a role as a steam valve to a straining system. "Sheer volume demands the use of screening devices in law enforcement. Official agencies are undermanned, underbudgeted, and overloaded; of necessity they must select for attention the cases that appear to them most pressing. The natural tendency appears to be to concentrate on major crimes, although there are exceptions and some choices are open to question." [17]

Hence, discretion and overload interact. Overload results, at least in part, from officials' hearty appetite for rescue, but in turn overload is kept in check by the exercise of discretion to screen out cases. Questions like why the ratio of informal to formal cases consistently remains about the same and what process equalizes the flow of children into detention with the number of available beds cannot authoritatively be answered. But they are well worth study. Efforts to change juvenile justice may falter if we do not master the workings of its component parts. The folklore of bureaucrats may shape juvenile justice more profoundly than exercises in political philosophy.

THE RECIPIENTS OF JUVENILE JUSTICE

But who is now swept up into the juvenile justice system? The largest number of cases disposed of by the courts in any given year are for delinquency. Over one million juvenile delinquency cases, excluding traffic offenses, were dealt with in 1970, and although the disparity between sexes is narrowing, boys still dominate the docket by a ratio of three to one (see Tables 7–1 and 7–2). About half a million of these "delinquency" cases involve status offenses or conduct: actions that are illegal for children only. Dependency and neglect cases handled by the courts totaled 133,000, or slightly more than 10 percent of all court cases (see Table 7–3). (This estimate includes adoption, child custody, termination of parental rights, and so on—cases that are heard in the juvenile courts of some, but by no means all, states.)

Delinquent conduct dominates the court's caseload, it is plain. But one can say very little about the type and seriousness of offenses. Data on police arrests offer some insight on the nonstatus offenses, because the police are the major source of referral. Commentary in the U.S. Department of Health, Education, and Welfare's *Juvenile Court Statistics, 1970,* contains these observations:

In the 1970 edition of Uniform Crime Reports, the Federal Bureau of Investigation reported that arrests of juveniles under 19 years of age, for all types of offenses combined, more than doubled between 1960 and 1970. For a group of serious offenses selected as being most reliably reported (criminal homicide, forcible rape, burglary, robbery, aggravated assault, larceny and auto theft), the combined increase between 1960 and 1970 was 95 percent. When offenses against the person (homicide, forcible rape, aggravated assault and robbery), generally accepted as being the most serious crimes, are selected from the reliably reported group, the increase between 1960 and 1970 was 167 percent.

As determined from police arrest data, all types of offenses— serious as well as relatively minor—are increasing, with the most serious ones showing substantially greater proportionate increases. Serious offenses against the person, however, still only represent about 3 *percent of all arrests of juveniles.*[18]

Thus, it appears reasonable to conclude: first, that delinquency cases have increased and, second, that the more serious offenses have increased somewhat more than the others.

TABLE 7–1

Delinquency Cases Disposed of by Juvenile Courts, by Sex, United States—1970

	TOTAL		BOYS		GIRLS	
Type of Court	Number of Cases	Percent of Total	Number of Cases	Percent of Total	Number of Cases	Percent of Total
Urban	686,000	66	512,500	64	173,500	69
Semiurban	296,800	28	233,500	29	63,300	25
Rural	69,200	6	53,500	7	15,700	6
Total	1,052,000	100	799,500	100	252,500	100

SOURCE: U.S. Department of Health, Education, and Welfare, *Juvenile Court Statistics, 1970* (National Center for Social Statistics Report, Juvenile Court Statistics, 1970).

TABLE 7–2

Delinquency Cases Disposed of by Courts, United States—1957–1970
(Numbers and Rate per 1,000 Children Age 10–17)

Year	Number of Cases	Child Population (10–17 Years of Age)	Rate
1957	440,000	22,173,000	19.8
1958	470,000	23,443,000	20.0
1959	483,000	24,607,000	19.6
1960	510,000	25,364,000	20.1
1961	503,000	26,029,000	19.3
1962	555,000	26,962,000	20.6
1963	601,000	28,031,000	21.4
1964	686,000	29,189,000	23.5
1965	697,000	29,479,000	23.6
1966	745,000	30,008,000	24.8
1967	811,000	30,750,000	26.4
1968	900,000	31,374,000	28.7
1969	988,500	31,971,000	30.9
1970	1,052,000	32,531,000	32.3

SOURCE: Same as Table 7–1. Data for 1957–1969 estimated from the national sample of juvenile courts. Data for 1970 estimated from all courts reporting whose jurisdictions included almost three-fourths of the population of the United States.

TABLE 7–3

Dependency and Neglect Cases Disposed of by Juvenile
Courts, United States—1970
(Numbers and Rates per 1,000 Children)

| | | RATE ° | | | |
| | | | Age Jurisdiction of Court | | |
Type of Court	Number of Cases	All Courts	Under 16	Under 17	Under 18 †
Urban	85,000	2.5	2.0	3.0	2.6
Semiurban	35,000	3.4	1.8	3.8	3.6
Rural	12,700	1.5	1.3	1.7	1.5

SOURCE: Same as Table 7–1. Based on the data from 1,595 courts
whose jurisdiction include about two-thirds of the child population
under 18 years of age.
° Calculated on the basis of the 1960 child population at risk, that
  is, the child population under 16, for courts whose age jurisdiction is under 16, etc.
† A small number of courts having jurisdiction of children under
  21 years of age are included here. The number of cases involved
  does not seriously affect the rates of the courts in this column.

These rather cautious conclusions do not support pronounce-
ments about the size or severity of delinquency, for we are
speaking only of reports of official activity. These do not measure illicit behavior per se, but only detected *and* recorded
misbehavior. When we scrutinize the steps that go into record making we might well conclude, along with Morris and
Hawkins, that clear information about delinquency trends
cannot be provided. These experts concluded that "such evidence as is available strongly suggests that the overall increase in juvenile delinquency can be largely, if not entirely,
attributed to the juvenile population increase." [19]

Before turning to reform proposals, we should say a word
about neglect and dependency. Informed observers believe a
screening process affects the volume and character of neglect
and dependency cases just as it affects the delinquency caseload. The types of influence that divert *offenders* from court

probably operate as forcefully upon neglect and dependency. Social agencies provide in some way for many of these children. Many cases can be dealt with consensually between child welfare agency and parent, obviating the necessity for judicial intervention. Many states permit government provision of substitute care without a formal judicial decree.

As with delinquency cases, however, we cannot discuss these cases with confidence. Without knowing the statutes, procedures, and services of each area, one cannot sort out cases in which the state adjudicates disputed issues from those in which the court is merely lending itself to social assistance. As the President's Commission on Law Enforcement noted, "Acting as a mere conduit for the referral of well-meaning people overwhelmed by life to a source of assistance for their economic ills is a burdensome task for any court, and one there is no need to handle judicially." [20]

Nevertheless, these points seem undebatable: neglect and dependency cases typically reflect severe current pathology and a history of inept efforts at intervention. These cases, even more than delinquency cases, appear to be concentrated in low-income families, and their clientele is recruited from social agency programs that are used primarily by the poor. Income usually makes the difference in involving courts in a private child care crisis. This is not to say that there are not disturbed, unhappy, or neglected children in middle- and upper-income homes. Common sense contends otherwise. But a family with economic resources turns to other sources of help instead of a court or related personnel. In any event, children coming before the court on neglect and dependency petitions are even more likely to be from poor families than are the children alleged to be delinquent.[21]

THE REFORM OF JUVENILE JUSTICE

Clearly, from what we have already said, juvenile courts may be criticized on numerous counts. Protecting the public is different from helping and rehabilitating juveniles or their parents. Acknowledgment of the fact that "the guiding consideration for a court of law that deals with threatening conduct is . . . protection of the community" would spare us from the delusion that when the state acts, it is invariably seeking to cure. We would also be spared the evils attendant on this delusion. One of these is inadequate procedure. It is too easy to be lulled into excusing lesser standards of due process for children—as if the court were "a hospital clinic and its only objective were to discover the child's malady and to cure him." [22]

Another evil is expansive grounds of jurisdiction, justified by the presumed causal chain between the vulnerability of infancy, the development of delinquent traits, and full-blown criminal delinquency. Such an extensive agenda creates overloads for the court which it has difficulty in reducing. If we accept the legitimacy of expansive authority in the abstract, then relatively modest offenses lay claim to judicial cognizance. There is no reason, in principle, to reject them. There is the possibility that courts that curb their appetites through self-denial can be accused of failing to protect children with sufficient vigor.

Juvenile court statistics appear to bear out this assertion. Roughly half of all cases handled do not involve *criminal* delinquent behavior. They are neglected and dependent children and children in need of supervision, as well as a few victims of delinquent criminal behavior. Many of the cases brought to court involve misconduct that is ubiquitous, for which referral to court must necessarily be highly discretionary. The sense of being "singled out" for behavior that is neither heinous nor rare can scarcely strengthen the juvenile's belief in an impartial system of justice. It violates his sense of proportion and of fairness. But, paradoxically, juvenile court intervention also has an opposite effect. Discretionary mitigation of penalties can be perceived as overleniency or naiveté, and this bores or annoys the older wards of court.[23] In this situation, referral to juvenile court violates the youth's self-esteem.

Where do we go from here? Contraction of legislative standards of intervention, introduction of procedural due process into juvenile courts, and diversion of official "cases" from the juvenile justice system at every point along the line have been suggested. Some have proposed eliminating child welfare cases altogether. This course may be necessary for substantial, long-lasting results.

The bulk of legal scholarship and landmark decisions of the Supreme Court [24] as well have emphasized the necessity of procedural change. Nonetheless, a few commentators clearly believe that radical surgery will be required if any of the changes in juvenile justice are to endure.[25]

There have been several specific moves to clarify the bases of intervention. Limiting delinquency to criminal behavior is widely favored. (Criminal law is itself not so narrow a spectrum!) The vital consequence of limiting delinquency to criminal behavior is twofold: the ability to set specific standards of due process for alleged juvenile offenders, just as for adult suspects; and the opportunity to relate penalties or court orders to the act, or acts, established. This approach leads naturally into questions of burden of proof, determination of fact, role of counsel, and need for jury trial, questions that inherit from the criminal law a commitment to adversarial process, our traditional way of keeping "benevolence" (or punitive impulse) in check.

Relating court orders to a strict definition of delinquency makes possible the clear identification of those forms of treatment or correction that are intended to protect the community. This does not preclude the possibility that treatment can occur (and should be sought) in corrective institutions. Nor does it rule out the obvious fact that, at any given time, "available means may be unsatisfactory when viewed either from the standpoint of the community interest or of the welfare of the delinquent child." [26] Redefining delinquency can eliminate the most coercive dispositional alternatives from those available in nondelinquent cases.[27]

Thus, juvenile court laws are being revised to differentiate among delinquents ("pure" law breakers), supervision cases (or the old "incorrigibles"), neglect and dependency. Although few courts and legislatures have yet extended right to counsel to parents (in neglect proceedings) or to both parent and child where they are in conflict, there is assuredly wider access to counsel today than ten years ago. The emergence of skilled legal counselors promises a considerable impact on law and policy.

To date, the major focus of litigation has been the adjudicatory and prepetition stages of juvenile justice. Questions have been raised concerning burden of proof, jury trial, and such police practices as placing juveniles in lineups and interrogating them without notification to parents or a *Miranda* warning. Statutory reform has also concentrated on these stages. But there are indications that more thought will be given to standards applicable to postadjudicatory treatment. The Illinois Unified Code of Corrections is one example of an effort to regularize the principles of humaneness and fairness in all correctional programs, juvenile programs included.[28]

This effort will doubtless find reinforcement in litigation over the next few years. And it is likely to generate a "lateral" movement aimed at practices in the more traditional areas of child welfare. Questioning the exercise of authority by correctional officials, where opportunities for abuse of power are most apparent, is basically an exercise in examining the limits of state power. Similar questions can be—and have been—addressed to the state acting "in behalf of" the neglected child. A dramatic example is found in recent litigation challenging the right of a state official, as guardian of the person of the minors involved, to control their stay in a mental hospital on voluntary commitment.[29] Of the several issues this case entails, one squarely posed is the low level of care—not to say, abusive type of care—that the juveniles were receiving in the hospital. "Right to treatment" questions will multiply, and their implications for traditional child welfare practice are as profound as they have been in mental health first, and now corrections.

If due process was the cry of reformers of juvenile justice at the outset of the 1960s, diversion is the password today. The two themes are intertwined. As demands for procedural formality multiply, pressure to divert cases from the system increases. Informal handling is cheaper than full-blown individualized justice. Moreover, the arguments that support due process in juvenile justice also support expansion of alternatives outside the justice system. The potential deprivation of freedom and the stigma inherent in court proceedings undergird the case for procedural regularity. Likewise, stigma and the overkill of formal process must be avoided in minor misbehaviors, reserving the ceremony and awesome power of formal proceedings for serious threats to community safety.

The notions of due process and diversion intersect in another way that is evident if we distinguish the ends of social control from child protection. Coercive authority is indispensable to social control. It is in the background, if not on stage fully visible, at every turning point in the process of official detection, weighing and adjudicating, and striving to correct. But the goals of child welfare are typically served by mediation and encouragement, by transfer of resources and creation of opportunities, through ombudsmen and social agencies, friends, and clergy. These objectives are best served when acceptance of aid is wholly voluntary. We may lose clients who will be unconvinced of their need for help or of the agency's ability to deliver it. But those we gain will presumably benefit.

With such a perspective, the President's Commission on Law Enforcement proposed a neighborhood agency to serve youth. This agency, while welcoming all comers, would be required to accept all police and court referrals. It would focus responsibility for types of cases that have been unpopular among child welfare agencies and the institutions, such as schools, that serve "normal" youths. The commission remarked:

A mandate for service seems necessary to insure energetic efforts to control and redirect acting-out youth and to minimize the substantial risk that this population, denied service by traditional agencies, will inevitably be shunted to a law enforcement agency.[30]

To date, the experience with such service—Youth Services Bureaus (YSBs)—has been disappointing. There are many questions about their sources of authority, means of support, professional tone, and relationships to other agencies.[31] "It is hard to escape the impression of old ideas being recycled," Edwin M. Lemert remarks, but he adds:

Diversion of children and youth from the official court system is a state of mind; once it is established as a predominant social value, the question of adaptation of means to the end should be more easily answered.[32]

And yet, if this were all there is to reforming juvenile justice, one might ask whether YSBs would not become the juvenile courts of the future. What would prevent the YSBs from harvesting the same stigmata and experiencing the same break-down between rhetoric and reality that have brought disapproval onto the heads of juvenile court officials? Are not the proponents of YSBs another generation of child savers in disguise, equipped with "hip" formulations that rest upon a subterranean reservoir of a "vast rhetoric of benevolence"? One can answer that any noncoercive helping mechanism may become freighted with a stigmatic aura and subtle forms of coercion. At any rate, the short-run gains might be worth the risk.

Simultaneously, we must sever the jurisdictional unity of the court, divorcing and contracting jurisdictional grounds. Let the juvenile court and all its officials be restricted to criminally delinquent behavior. In addition, let noncriminal misbehavior and neglect cases find a forum other than a juvenile court. The aim is, first, to divert nondelinquency cases from courts altogether and, second, to avoid mixing them with delinquency cases where, in the end, judicial action is required. This approach will reduce contact at the slippery edges of jurisdictional categories. Neglect and delinquency petitions, to illustrate, could not simply be converted one into the other in the midst of case processing.

This is necessary if the desired contraction of jurisdiction is to be achieved. The most rigorous definitions of neglect and incorrigibility are still very broad indeed; official action may be hard to contain. Clear-cut identification of the juvenile court with juvenile crime will set straight the minds of all as to who are appropriately referred to it. A resource like YSBs for other types of misbehavior would likewise serve to push forward the point Lemert asserts: that diversion is a state of mind.

The procedural protections that evolve in delinquency litigation need not automatically apply to other types of cases. We might prefer to reshape neglect proceedings closely to resemble administrative hearings, with court review limited in scope. To this end we could emphasize voluntary services and reserve judicial review for the most stubborn problem situations. Court review might be reserved for appeals or for cases of major curtailment of parental rights. Doubtless, different patterns should be encouraged so that we may learn from experience which models are most efficient and protective of individual rights.

Reform appears to lie in two directions—perfection of the due-process model of juvenile justice in criminal delinquency cases, and perfection of a several-tiered administrative model for child welfare cases. Judicial sanctions in the latter instance could not be entirely eliminated, but, one would hope, they would be severely pruned. The cloak of benevolence that now justifies the informal conduct and expansive appetite of the juvenile justice system must be withdrawn. The presumption of legitimate authority to intervene has been fostered by the system's jurisdictional "unity," and the operational burden of proof has too often fallen on the individual to show that he has not erred.

The lesson of the 1960s is that shifting this burden will not be achieved merely through changes in rhetoric or the introduction of new actors, such as lawyers.[33] The processes of juvenile justice, complexly interwoven as they are, defy simple solutions. A change in expectations is required. We owe it to juvenile officials to protect them from their own zeal and from the castigation of an over-zealous public. Narrowed jurisdictional grounds and differential mechanisms are two ways to make clear that our expectations are different from those the child savers cherished.

It is not that we care less for children and youths today. It is simply that, having tried rescue, we are cautious about even well-motivated state action, and we suspect, in contrast to our forebears, that doing less is doing more.

NOTES

1. President's Commission on Law Enforcement and Administration of Justice, *The Challenge of Crime in a Free Society* (Washington, D.C.: Government Printing Office, 1967).
2. Alfred J. Kahn, "Court and Community," in *Justice for the Child*, ed. Margaret K. Rosenheim (New York: Free Press, 1962), pp. 217–234.
3. Norval Morris and Gordon Hawkins, *The Honest Politician's Guide to Crime Control* (Chicago: University of Chicago Press, 1970), p. 157.
4. Morris and Hawkins, *Honest Politician's Guide*, p. 159.
5. Oscar L. Dudley, "Saving the Children: Sixteen Years' Work Among the Dependent Youth of Chicago," in *History of Child-Saving in the United States*, National Conference of Charities and Correction, Committee on the History of Child-Saving Work (Boston: The Conference, 1893), p. 99.
6. Monrad G. Paulsen, "The Constitutional Domestication of the Juvenile Court," in *1967 Supreme Court Review*, Philip B. Kurland, ed. (Chicago: University of Chicago Press, 1967), p. 242 quoting Julian W. Mack, "The Juvenile Court," *Harvard Law Review*, 23 (1909), 104, 116–117.
7. Morris and Hawkins, *Honest Politician's Guide*, pp. 157–158.
8. Francis A. Allen, *The Borderland of Criminal Justice* (Chicago: University of Chicago Press, 1964), pp. 51–54.
9. Jane Addams, *My Friend, Julia Lathrop* (New York: Macmillan, 1935), p. 137.
10. *The Challenge of Crime*, p. 86.
11. Nicholas D. Kittrie, *The Right to Be Different: Deviance and Enforced Therapy* (Baltimore: Johns Hopkins Press, 1970).
12. Morris and Hawkins, *Honest Politician's Guide*, p. 165.
13. *The Challenge of Crime*, p. 80.
14. Morris and Hawkins, *Honest Politician's Guide*, p. 158.
15. *Kent* v. *United States*, 383 U.S. 541 (1966).
16. Joel F. Handler and Margaret K. Rosenheim, "Privacy in Welfare: Public Assistance and Juvenile Justice," *Law and Contemporary Problems*, 31 (Spring 1966), 377.
17. *Task Force Report: Juvenile Delinquency and Youth Crime*, p. 10. Kenneth C. Davis, *Discretionary Justice* (Baton Rouge: Louisiana State University Press, 1969).
18. U.S. Department of Health, Education, and Welfare, *Juvenile Court Statistics, 1970* (National Center for Social Statistics Report, Juvenile Court Statistics, 1970), p. 3. Italics added.

19. Morris and Hawkins, *Honest Politician's Guide,* p. 151.
20. *Task Force Report: Juvenile Delinquency and Youth Crime,* p. 28.
21. See Nanette Dembitz, "The Good of the Child Versus the Rights of the Parent: The Supreme Court Upholds the Welfare Home-Visit," *Political Science Quarterly,* 86 (September 1971), 389.
22. *The Challenge of Crime,* p. 81.
23. Elliott Studt, "The Client's Image of the Juvenile Court," in *Justice for the Child,* ed. Margaret K. Rosenheim (New York: Free Press, 1962), p. 209.
24. *Kent* v. *United States,* 383 U.S. 541 (1966); *In re Gault,* 387 U.S. 1 (1967); *Debacker* v. *Brainard,* 396 U.S. 28 (1969); *In re Winship,* 397 U.S. 358 (1970); *McKeiver* v. *Pennsylvania,* 403 U.S. 528 (1971).
25. Morris and Hawkins, *Honest Politician's Guide,* p. 156.
26. Allen, *The Borderland of Criminal Justice,* p. 53.
27. Illinois Revised Statutes, c. 37, 705–2(1)(b) (1972).
28. See, generally, Illinois Revised Statutes, c. 38, 1003 (1972).
29. *Chicago Sun Times,* August 25, 1972, p. 76.
30. *The Challenge of Crime,* p. 83.
31. Margaret K. Rosenheim, "Youth Services Bureaus: A Concept in Search of Definition," *Juvenile Court Judges Journal,* 20 (Spring 1969), 69–74; J. A. Seymour, "Youth Services Bureaus," *Law and Society Review,* 7 (1972), 247.
32. Edwin M. Lemert, *Instead of Court,* Crime and Delinquency Issues (Chevy Chase, Md.: National Institute of Mental Health, 1971), pp. 93–95.
33. Anthony M. Platt, *The Child Savers: The Invention of Delinquency* (Chicago: University of Chicago Press, 1969), pp. 101–136.

8

Poor Care for Poor Children — What Way Out?

ALVIN L. SCHORR

There it is. Organized programs for children turn out, when examined, to be programs for the poor, for blacks, and for the otherwise disadvantaged. There is no harm in that alone; it might be a good thing if the programs were good, but the programs are poor. Foster families and institutions are a dead end for children who use them more than a few months—and perhaps half of the children do. There is even "greater difficulty in implementing plans for care of the child in his own home. . . ." [1] Most day care is custodial in nature, despite all the talk about quality. Juvenile and family courts detain, treat, and punish children who, if their families were wealthier, would not have been brought to court. Health care of children is fragmented, often impersonal, and at times ineffective or even inappropriate.

WHO DOES BETTER?

The broad statement that organized children's programs serve poor children overlooks internal distinctions and exceptions. Child welfare includes several distinct systems of day care. There is a fine system for a trivial number of the poor and disadvantaged, and custodial care for a larger number of the poor. The marginally poor, if they use day care, pay for it in proprietary centers. Children of the middle classes use none of these systems. Almost all use some form of care, but they rely on unpaid or paid help in or near the home. Thus, we understand why the poor complain that they cannot find day care while newspapers describe model day care centers.

One sees somewhat different internal distinctions in institutional care. Institutions for the dependent and neglected are largely occupied by the poor, and institutions for detention and punishment almost solely so. By contrast, middle-class families want residential psychiatric treatment for their children but cannot afford its full cost. Consequently, those particular children's institutions are heavily populated by middle-class children at reduced cost or at no cost to the parents. It is not that poor children do not need psychiatric treatment as much as other care. We have seen that institutional staffs and outpatient psychiatric clinics diagnose them as needing treatment and leave it at that.

Adoption is another exception to the rule—a troubling if not indeed illuminating exception. Apart from children adopted by their own relatives, most adopted children are illegitimate and from poor parents. (Not from the very poorest parents, studies seem to indicate, many of whom seem to have solved their problem with neglect or—even before legalization—do-it-yourself abortion.) On the other hand, adoptive parents tend not to be poor at all. As one study puts

it, adoptive children experience "upward social mobility." [2]
So one might say that adoption agencies are a system for re-
distributing children from the poor to the middle classes. We
note, for example, that abortion was denied to the poor for
years—from 1960 to 1965, 42 percent of births to the poor
and near-poor were unwanted, compared with 17 percent
among the nonpoor.[3] And in those years, although the practice was urged and tried out here and there, most agencies
would not place black and other minority children with
white families for adoption. But the birthrate was declining,
and abortion became more widely available; a severe shortage of children for adoption developed. *Then* interracial
adoption took hold. It is difficult to test cause and effect; still,
the supply provided by the poor was made to respond to the
demand for children among the nonpoor (and, in the process,
a small sector of discrimination fell away). Though they were
wrong in principle, one understands the rage of militant
black social workers who took a stand against interracial
adoption.[4]

The exceptions may prove a broader rule. Child welfare is
a generally poor system for poor children, but the nonpoor
use it to their advantage when the payoff is sufficiently important. They use residential psychiatric treatment centers
and, for similar reasons, outpatient psychiatric treatment.
They use adoption services as consumers, though not widely
as suppliers. It is significant that among the wide range of
child welfare programs, these are the very ones that have established high quality and high status.

One other peculiarity of the class-linked nature of child
welfare services seems worth noting. Each chapter of this
book complains about the paucity of data on the class background of child welfare children. Institutional care has been
extensively surveyed, but not all the volumes of reports manage to deal directly with the incomes of families from which

the children come. In the nature of the way medical care is provided for poor children, one knows their income level by definition. On the other hand, information that would be necessary to compare the quality of their medical care with that of other children is wholly absent. We know that poor children die for lack of any care at all; [5] little more than that. In 1967, scholars concluded a careful review of European and American research on child welfare services; the indexes of their reports do not contain the words "class," "social class," or "economic class." [6] Few experts are really in doubt about the conclusions to which indirect evidence has brought us here, but researchers have been resolutely class-blind. It is as if there is something there we do not want to know.

THE PRICE OF POOR PROGRAMS

Children involved in the child welfare system pay a price that is visible; earlier chapters catalog these costs. Children do not eat properly; their physical ills may be diagnosed but not treated; they live in crowded and unsanitary housing. They are separated from their natural parents, but real parental responsibility is not accepted anywhere. As a result of these problems, they come to school developmentally and socially unprepared. They are kept in institutions when they should be in foster family homes. They are kept in foster family care when they should be in their own homes. They are moved from one placement to another, "and replacements and maladjustments increase together." [7] They are labeled delinquent, though every expert knows that keeping them out of courts and institutions would be better all around, and are tracked into antisocial behavior. They pay a price all their lives, both psychologically and in their careers.

A point of ideology underlies the damage that is done to poor children in programs limited to them. We have seen that in other countries institutional care of children may work out very well. For example, a study of children reared in Austrian Kinderdorfen, Israeli Kibbutzim, and Polish and Yugoslav children's homes concludes that they—in contrast to American institutions—are successful. The essential difference is a firm belief in the children's capacities and a general conviction that they will succeed.[8] Similarly, children emerge far better equipped from our private boarding schools (patronized by our middle classes) than from our child welfare institutions. It is the fact of separate systems itself that establishes the initial expectation of failure or success. With the expectation settled, the type of personnel attracted and the necessary policies fall into line, and the children obligingly fulfill expectations.

Closely related is the professional assumption that child welfare children and families tend to require professional treatment. If one defines the need for child welfare as unique to a poor (read "emotionally troubled," not to say "culpable") portion of the population, naturally they would seem to require professional treatment. Moreover, the definition is tested from day to day by professionals who are trained to the need for treatment. However, "the whole model of treatment and rehabilitation of family and child is unsupportable." [9] In practice comparatively little professional treatment is given. And it is difficult to demonstrate that professional treatment alters the outcome for children.[10] For example, we have noted that children in foster care because their mothers have an acute illness, and so forth, are likely to return home quickly, while children placed for reasons related to the need for professional treatment are likely to remain in care indefinitely.

The treatment assumption converts what should be public

issues (how to provide housing so families will not be dispersed, for example) into private problems (how to treat a marital problem).[11] Its insidious quality is that it supports the ideology of failure. While a child welfare worker focuses on specialized treatment facilities that are generally not available, simple needs—a few hours of adult care in the neighborhood, eyeglasses and dental care, enough money for food and shelter—are not provided. Parents are eventually lost to sight, to be sure, and children show all the symptoms of deep disturbance that have been expected. The assumption of an emotionally troubled poor population then turns out to be accurate and supports the view that the child welfare programs which they populate will chiefly graduate failures.

WHAT DETERMINES HOW MUCH WE DO?

No one works very long in child welfare without experiencing the feeling of being a cog in some giant homeostatic mechanism. Are foster family homes in desperately short supply? A public campaign is launched, and additional homes secured —but not nearly enough. Do families yield up their own children because AFDC payments are below the survival, let alone the poverty, level? Arguments from humanity are foregone; rather, the point is put that a child in foster family care costs $4,400 a year.[12] (AFDC payments for a child average only about $600 a year.) AFDC payments may then rise slightly, but not in any reasonable relationship to the apparent economy of supporting children at home.

These pleas of desperation and arguments about relative cost are made from the wrong premise, for no one expects all or a large proportion of need to be met. (The professional learns from bitter experience not to expect it; in time he comes to settle for very little. Inexperienced observers see him as part of the problem, and they are right, of course.) Legislators and administrators are willing to spend extravagant amounts of money per child because they do not intend at any time to care for all the children who are said to require it. (Meanwhile, extravagance per child is offered in evidence of public responsibility and generosity.) The structure of the system provides its own rationing device.[13] In a system for poor children, the first limit reached is the amount of money that the nation is willing at any given time to spend on poor children. The *requirements* of poor children are not in focus at all, let alone the requirements of children in general.

If confining poor children to a special, poor system of care is a rationing system, the development of services will move by fad and passing generous impulse and have little connection with actual requirements. All the studies and commission findings are useless: everyone assumes that need will be said to be far in excess of services provided; everyone understands that little will be done. Children's advocates will offer a bald claim for a nationwide system of psychiatric treatment centers for children, which the opposition will ignore or categorically reject. Voices will get shriller, and the antagonists will not hear each other. One has only to consult his experience to confirm this.

In short, a system that is limited to poor children can deal with some unspecified portion of the need without greatly troubling the nation. That may be its function. If the welfare of all of our children or of the children of influential parents were at stake, provision would respond more sensitively to need. But most of those children have their needs met in other ways not called child welfare. Still, there must be nonpoor children who are unable for one reason or another (because even moderate income is not adequate to the cost, because a family lacks relatives or friends nearby) to use alternative middle-class systems. There is no room for them in the child welfare programs. In any event, their parents understand that entering the system means failure and avoid it if at all possible. Such children must be numbered in the millions, and they also go without care. They reflect one cost to the nonpoor of the manner in which we deal with the poor.

Another cost to the nonpoor lies in the spread by contagion of practices that are permitted in a poor people's system. Chapter 7 shows that our juvenile and family courts operate with widespread disregard for the basic legal rights of children—partly out of a therapeutic orientation and partly because those particular children cannot defend themselves. Courts have spread their authority beyond any reasonable precedent and without safeguards, such as an adversary procedure, that have been embedded in our law. Those rights, if and when they are lost, are lost for all children. Moreover, the understanding by poor children on one hand and the nonpoor on the other that they are subject to the law largely in relation to their families' wealth and influence spreads disrespect for courts everywhere. Justice is either blind or not; half-blind is a wink.

There are other costs of separate programming for poor children, of course. The deepening of evident schisms and of class hostility that is surprisingly sharp for a society said to be classless must be terribly dangerous. But such effects are conjectural, and we will not dwell on them.

HOW DID WE GET INTO THIS?

We have seen that, historically and in common law, the sources of public concern for children lie with dependent, which is to say poor, children. By 1912, Congress at any rate charged the U.S. Children's Bureau with concern for children "among all classes of our people," but reformers remained preoccupied with poor children. It was not until the 1930s that—in social security legislation that made a number of fundamental departures—so called universal patterns of service, cutting across class lines, were broadly laid down.

At that point we departed from dealing with children (and people) who could demonstrate poverty and undertook in our programs to deal with all who were orphaned, unemployed, aged, and so forth. As a consequence, millions of children now receive social security benefits without regard to family income, children who, by previous patterns, would be forced to apply for AFDC or would receive nothing. Social service and health programs that were enacted for children in the same period also tended to be universal in principle, that is, they were directed to all children in a defined group (survivors, crippled, living in rural areas) without regard to income.

Although cash social security flourished and took wing, social service and health programs unfortunately remained small. By the 1970s, various health programs for children (Medicaid apart) provided comprehensive service to only a million children and special services to a million more. The opposition of organized medicine to these programs was certainly a factor in keeping them small. Organized social work also opposed expansion of social services beyond the capacity of trained professionals to staff them, and that proved to be not very fast. (It has to be said for organized social work, in contrast to organized medicine, that it did earnestly try to expand the number of trained social workers.) Although a structure for universal child welfare programs was established across the country, by 1960 leaders had to acknowledge that "the goals which must be reached if the needs of children are to be met are still distant." [14] Child welfare programs remained relatively small; without the quantum jump that would have been required for change, they continued to be largely devoted to poor children.[15]

It has been argued that countries adopt universal policies at times of national crisis that knit populations together.[16] Social security programs were laid down during and following the 1929 depression. With growing distance from that period, we have drifted away from universal programs. In their place in the 1960s, there was a flowering of the so-called selective programs that require that people prove themselves poor in order to receive benefits. The war on poverty confirmed and accentuated a trend that was already perceptible. In the past decade, even cash payments in social security have been skewed to give an increasing proportion to people not poor,[17] with growing numbers expected to apply to the selective program called public assistance. Child welfare services, universal at least in intention, were being whittled away and replaced, if at all, by services tied to income— AFDC services.

It is a bitter but important point that the more emphatically programs are confined to poor children, the smaller the likelihood that the trend will be reversed. It is well understood sociologically that institutions with low-status clients have low-status professionals, and vice versa. We have seen that the background and status of workers in foster family care and institutions reflect this status link between client and worker. The employees in these programs carry low status *level for level*, that is executives compared with other executives, professionals with other kinds of professionals, and so forth. These toilers in the vineyard of disadvantaged clients tend, therefore, to carry little weight politically. They are not an effective force in getting the programs improved.

Speaking more broadly, the quality of children's programs, like others, depends on the power of a political constituency that can be mustered to keep them well financed and administered. But a series of developments are accentuating the competition for public funds, even as the country grows wealthier. Public debate about relative income status of various groups—the poor, blue collar, middle classes—has been defined in such a fashion as to create the impression that all are losing ground. Each fights harder for its own advantage and, among other effects, secures reductions in tax rate. Certain groups—dependent children and the aged in particular —grow in numbers and, by existing legislation, require heavier commitment of public funds. And a continuous commitment to war or defense draws heavily. In the long, intense competition for tax dollars that is inevitable, poor people without allies do not make out well. So even children's programs that have started out brave and fine deteriorate over time. Poor services, the treatment assumption, the expectation of failure, and poor results tend then to be ascribed to the endowment or character of the children and their parents rather than to the character of the system that contains them. What *can be* is judged by what *is*—the juvenile and family courts we have discussed, the crowded institutions and day care centers, the waiting rooms in hospitals and clinics. The programs are poor because they are separate, but parents and legislators, seeking better programs, are doubly persuaded that they must be separate.

One perceives in this brief outline that we are profoundly committed by history and inclination to dealing with poor children separately. Universal public education is one strand that cuts across this pattern—so deeply rooted in the American ethos that it has not centrally been subject to attack. Universal social security is another eccentric strand, begun in the depression and a perhaps inevitable product of insecurity that comes with industrialization. Social security is being chipped away at as a universal program, but perhaps it is also impregnable. That cannot be said of the cash, health, and social service programs for children we consider here. There have been moments when we seemed to move away from duplex programming—one set of programs for the poor and another set for the others. Each time we were overwhelmed by history and by the forces that lead such programming, once set in motion, to perpetuate itself.

HOW CAN IT BE!

We began with the recognition that, although we are in some sense a child-centered country, a strain of hostility to children colors our attitudes and policies. Apart from this, children have historically been treated "as a private venture for the sake of personal satisfaction." [18] Recent debate about population growth has displayed very clearly the view that children are a personal indulgence and public policy should not relieve the burden of families in having them. Over the longer run as well, a largely Protestant electorate has suspected that policies that favor children are pro-Catholic. Therefore, the tendency has been to avoid confrontation on programs that directly benefit large numbers of children. (Public education came to the brink of financial catastrophe before federal aid to education could be enacted. There has been more than enough confrontation over desegregation and busing, but few suppose that the central issue is children.) The effect of regarding children as a private venture is that it is difficult to organize politically around their interests. One can name a number of potent national organizations that represent the aged, or veterans, or the disabled, but none of the groups interested in children is powerful in the same degree.

In short, those who are interested in children are not powerful politically because the nation is ambivalent about its children and because deeper policy cleavages divide those who might otherwise join together for children. Yet one would expect that a dramatic issue such as hunger among children or instances of child abuse would produce lasting and powerful response.

Indeed, there are responses. We then see a problem that has become general in recent years: we cannot make institutions responsive to our desires even with new money and new ideas. The new efforts are swallowed up in a fundamental policy choice of which the public and policy makers remain virtually unconscious—the choice to invest in programs limited to poor children. For example, in a series of increasingly emphatic pieces of legislation—in 1956, 1962, and 1967—Congress has insisted that certain kinds of services should be made available to AFDC families. These services were never really rendered, as we have seen, and one of the reasons is that poor people's programs do not in their nature command delivery of quality services. But Congress and the public are not attentive to the fundamental policy choice that is implicit here. All that is clear is that they are willing to invest in children; indeed, they insist that money be spent; and the matter turns out badly.

We may now hazard a direct answer to the question. How can it be that children are abused, or neglected, or starved, or exploited, and decent people do no better? First, we are not wholly decent. If this comes as a surprise to us, we should face it. We love our children and do much for them, but we do not love them all or in every circumstance, and often we turn on them angrily *because* they are in difficulty. Second, when we do attempt to serve them, we find ourselves politically divided, and other issues (demographic, religious, racial, and professional) become more important than the outcome for children. Third, possibly without intending it, we have perfected a system that rations service and contains its own adulterated standards of performance. By focusing on services rendered—how much they cost and whether they are increasing—rather than on who needs to be served, we escape full knowledge that we might do better. A consistent absence of research data relating class to quality of service or who is served abets ignorance. Fourth, we are for various reasons committed to duplex programming. The system joins relatively low-status professionals to low-status clients, as if designed for impotence. The system works out badly—a point to which we resolutely do not pay attention—and leaves vaguely confirmed a feeling that the problems are inevitable. We cannot help, so it must be right that we should not help.

The reader who takes this as a fatalistic statement fails to understand it. These particular institutions, at any rate, seem unresponsive because we have not taken pains to understand the implicit choices we were making and, when we sought to make changes, have not had the tenacity to follow through. Fatalism is as fatalism does.

UNIVERSAL PROGRAMMING FOR CHILDREN

We have been so deeply committed to duplex programming that universal services for children may be difficult to visualize. Illustrations may help, in order to provide something of the shape and feel of universal services. Because AFDC has become so prominent a problem, we begin with income maintenance for children.

On the whole, children have been getting a declining share of what is paid out in social security. That is, if one divides the share of social security paid out in 1950 and 1970 between families with children and families without children, it turns out that the children's share has been declining. (The reasons include the greater political effectiveness of the aged in improving their benefits and the development of new programs for adults—chiefly Medicare.) In pursuing universal programming, one would set out to improve the share of children in social security.

For example, the families of orphaned children cannot receive payments in excess of a maximum related to the father's earnings record. As a result, in low- and moderate-income families, second or third children who have been orphaned may fail to receive any benefits at all. A modest change would provide benefits to 700,000 children who have been excluded. Similarly, because of unduly rigorous requirements, only about a quarter of severely disabled adults receive social security payments. Liberalization of this law has been recommended by the statutory Advisory Council on Social Security. Many of the families that would be extended benefits include children.

Long overdue is a federal program of unemployment insurance for those who have been unable to find work for more than six months. (A state-federal system provides benefits for up to six months.) In 1971, two million such workers used the full six months of unemployment compensation and then turned, perforce, to special emergency programs or welfare. These are predominantly middle-aged heads of families with children. With long years of work behind them, they are victims of technological or economic displacement. By the time they have received unemployment compensation for six months, they have exhausted reserves and plainly need new skills and special help in finding work. We need for them a federal unemployment insurance program that would be closely linked to retraining and job placement.

Such expansions and perfections of social security would provide support to families for millions of children. Analysis indicates that, given unemployment below 5 percent, families that include as many as six or eight million children would remain in need. Besides, wiping out need at poverty levels is not sufficient. Public debate in recent years has uncovered a disposition to relieve need at intermediate levels—for the so-called working poor. (Help for the working poor is essentially help for families with several children. That is, a working man or woman earns at minimum wage almost enough to bring a family of four to the poverty level. Thus, proposed supplementation is largely for families with two or more children.)

In attempting to face this problem, the electorate was occupied during the 1960s and early 1970s with various selective schemes—guaranteed income, negative income tax, and President Nixon's Family Assistance Plan.[19] Whatever their differences in detail, all would have made a payment dependent on the family's level of income and been limited to the very poor. But universal programs directed to cash needs of children could accomplish the same objectives for the working poor and others in need. A number of proposals with somewhat different rationales have been put forward over the years.

The children's allowance is the oldest type of proposal. Introduced in Europe at the end of the nineteenth century, it was used by employers to keep wages down (that is, to pay heads of large families enough for their minimum needs without raising the wages of others) and by governments to encourage a higher birthrate. With the growing strength of labor unions and other economic changes, children's allowances proved ineffective in restraining wage increases, and they never influenced birthrates noticeably.[20]

Children's allowances across western Europe and in Canada have grown and been strengthened since the 1950s, in pursuit of a rather different objective. Wage patterns and family patterns are out of phase in modern industrial economies. Typically, a wage earner earns little at the time he is 20 or 25 and increases his income into his middle years. His wife earns little or nothing in the first few years of marriage, when she is occupied with young children. She may go to work when the youngest enters school and is really free to work when the children are teenagers or out of the home. Thus, there is a shortage of money in households in the very years when children are growing up. Later, when the children are on their own, there may be a relative surplus. It would be useful if a family could draw on the income it will have later to expand resources in the first years of marriage. Apart from this, large families have the hardest time of all, of course. (Sixty percent of poor children are members of families with four or more children.) A nation with a stake in children, while it need not meet the full cost of raising children, will make some contribution that equalizes the burden as between large and small families.

A program of children's allowances is simple to outline. Cong. Donald Fraser's proposal would pay $600 a year to parents for every child under 18. At the same time, it would wipe out the income tax exemption for children.[21] No one would lose under the proposal, but obviously the rich, who benefit most from tax exemptions, would gain less than the poor. Young families with children would receive a government payment; in return, they would find themselves paying higher taxes when their own income is higher and the children leave home. Families with several children would receive a government contribution of $600 per child toward the cost of raising them. As an indication of impact, such a program would halve the AFDC caseload immediately and would do a great deal more for the working poor than the Family Assistance Plan that Congress considered in 1971 and 1972.[22]

A second, more sweeping rationale for a universal program that would affect children was proposed in Great Britain, in 1942, by Lady Rhys-Williams. She proposed a far-reaching redistribution of income and an implicit contract between the individual and the state, the former responsible for production and the latter for assuring income.[23] This would be accomplished by a flat income grant to all citizens, supplemented by social security payments for particular purposes. Such a proposal was advanced in the United States during the presidential campaign of Senator George McGovern.[24] At $1,000 per person, it proved to be inordinately expensive and was withdrawn. In any event, the principle goes beyond a children's allowance—which would *share* the expense of *child rearing*—to guarantee *minimum income for all*.

Between 1942 and 1972, Britain took a route much like the United States. Social security expanded and then in the 1960s gave way to selective programs. A program similar to the welfare reform that was rejected in the United States was in fact enacted in Britain. There ensued a good deal of dissatisfaction with selectivity (experience showed that many would not apply for benefits defined as limited to poor people) and a desire to simplify a system of taxes and payments that was becoming impossibly complex. In 1972, the British government proposed a system of tax credits that might have been modeled on Lady Rhys-Williams' proposal, but at a modest payment level.[25]

In short, a need for modest redistribution, the failures of selectivity in practice, and the increasing complexities of the tax and welfare system brought the British government to design a universal system. We could well take a similar step in the United States, for the background is the same.

In this country, tax exemptions favor those who are wealthier. That is, a $750 personal exemption is worth nothing to a poor person, $150 to an average taxpayer, and $375 to the wealthy person who pays tax at a 50 percent rate. So much has selectivity failed that Congress was not able in three years to agree on a welfare reform bill, despite widespread conviction that some change was necessary. And various income maintenance and tax measures interrelate in so complex a manner as to be beyond general understanding and, in many cases, counterproductive.[26] To correct these problems, one would eliminate the $750 income tax exemption and replace it with a tax credit or cash payment of $250 to every person. The credit would be reduced by 5 percent of income in excess of $6,000 a year, but no one would benefit less than he does with present income tax exemptions. The net cost would be about $10 billion, about half of it going to families with incomes of less than $5,000 a year, and the other half concentrated in the $5,000 to $15,000 income bracket. As it is a payment per person and as families with more children are concentrated in the lower income brackets, obviously it would greatly benefit children.

Among other proposals are the mother's wage—that is, to regard housework and child rearing as socially useful work and to pay a government wage for it [27]—and social security payments to children whose parents separate or divorce, just as they are now made to children whose parents die.[28] None of the principles for universal programs has been developed here in sufficient detail for a thoughtful choice among them. They are identified to show that other rationales than poverty would provide income to children. In their nature, some rationales would funnel money relatively effectively to the very families who would otherwise be poor. This is quite the situation that was intended and achieved by current social security programs. If we want universal income maintenance programs, the ideas are at hand.

UNIVERSAL HEALTH AND SOCIAL SERVICES

We have seen that the government provides inferior medical care to some children at a cost that would provide comprehensive care to all children, if services were rationally organized. This makes the case for integrating government health services, but those are now largely selective and inevitably would run the risk of being poor services. Dr. Julius Richmond has put the case for going further:

A more nearly universal system, with equal access to health services for the nation's children, would go far to ameliorate the problems and consequences of childhood disease among the rich and the poor. Fundamental conceptual changes in the nature of the delivery of child health services would include entitlement. . . .

The several options for the site of preventive child health services include the health-care system itself, child care institutions, and the welfare structures. Irrespective of where the screening and preventive care for children takes place, however, its *universality* is a primary goal. There is no particular reason to insist on one delivery structure over another.[29]

The issue of universal health care goes deeper than the question of how care should be financed. If poor people are paid for in one system and others in another, little is likely to have been achieved. But the issue of universality is quite sharply drawn even in the proposals for financing that have been presented to the electorate. The National Health Insurance Partnership Act, sponsored for the Nixon Administration by Senator Wallace F. Bennett and Congressman John W. Byrnes, would establish two plans, one for employed persons and one for low-income people. By contrast, the Health Security Act, offered by Senator Edward Kennedy and Congresswoman Martha Griffiths, would establish a single plan covering everyone. One may see an indication of the direction in which the duplex Administration plan might develop in a single pair of provisions. Those covered as employed population would receive maternity benefits. The low-income population would not receive maternity benefits, but family planning services instead.

Issues in the social services for children are similar. For a decade, the main thrust of day care legislation has been to link it to the needs of welfare mothers, who may in effect be required to use it or lose assistance. We have seen that existing provision for day care—conceived in terms of poor children—is largely limited to congregate care and is unrelated to the way families live and want to live. So much was the focus on expanding congregate care that staff were sidetracked from preventing quite serious abuses in existing centers. In the same period, a so-called Comprehensive Child Development Act would have provided funding at the rate of $2 billion a year for a flexible array of services—congregate day care, day care in and near the home, educational services, nutritional services, and so forth. All children would have been served. This proposal promised to break out of the selective mold and carried funding sufficient to establish a new pattern. Congress passed the bill and the president vetoed it with a message that stated the issue clearly: neither the need nor desirability of a national program had been demonstrated, he said. He preferred a smaller program linked to welfare.

It may be evident that we can review each type of care—institutions, foster family homes, outpatient psychiatric clinics, child welfare services (versus AFDC services)—illustrating the issue between universal and selective programming. In a few cases, middle-class children monopolize public services of good quality; the problem is to see that poor children get to use them. In most cases, programs are so identified with poor people as not to be salvageable for purposes of a universal system. They must be phased out and ways devised to include poor people in the systems now used by middle-class children. Some parts of this middle-class system are not organized facilities at all. They rest on being able to buy help in the private market or on access to family members with energy and time to spend. Services that substitute for these resources—homemakers, mother's helpers, family vacations—are well understood here and abroad, but not widely available in the United States. In seeking to move to a single but more diversified system for the care of children, such substitute services would be greatly expanded.

One may worry—certainly the planners of the poverty program worried—that poor people will not gain access to universal programs. They may get their legal share of cash under programs of social security, children's allowances, or tax credits, but health and personal social services—which are always in short supply—flow to those who are able to command them. It is a problem that should be borne in mind. Continuous review and evaluation of programs to avoid "creaming" is desirable. It is desirable also to build in administrative devices (outreach services, citizen participation, advocacy arrangements) that assure that all who are entitled to help are reached.

Moreover, there may be moments or situations in which a selective program is desirable; that need not be heresy. For example, so complex a society as ours will probably always need a relatively small welfare program to deal with exceptional situations. We have not intended here to dwell on details, but on whether the main direction of children's services is selective or universal. It is the central direction, not the details, that creates the present picture of children's services.

Contemporary science fiction, unable to outpace technological development, has grown quite sociological. Many stories deal with desperate attempts to understand a world in which everything seems commonplace but some simple assumption is unstated. The space traveler thinks he has a soul; the Martian thinks not. Here individual life is all; there the concept of life is vested in the community. Interplanetary wars are fought until some child or poet stumbles on the key. The situation in child welfare is not dissimilar. There are many problems and choices we understand; for better or worse, we are responsible for them. But selectivity is laid on us by a history that may no longer be functional; it is maintained by its own tendency to perpetuate itself; on the whole we have not even known we were making a choice. Unfortunately, selectivity means war, and the losers are always the same—children and the poor.

We should not end on a note of seeming simplicity. If we move services for children toward universality, we shall spend more on children and change our attitudes toward poverty and children as well. Profound forces move in this direction. Analyzing the shortcomings of the war on poverty, Richard Titmuss put the challenge as follows:

The "War on Poverty," despite its radicalism and its unorthodoxies of "opting out" of the power structure, has not found the answers to the challenge of how to provide benefits in favour of the poor without stigma. What makes this problem of redistribution such a formidable challenge today—both in Britain and the USA—is that it is now inextricably mixed up with the challenge of social rights as well as civil rights for "coloured" citizens. Two standards of service, in quality and methods of administration, one for the black and one for the white, are now seen to be more intolerable to the public conscience than two standards of service for the poor and the non-poor.[30]

That is to say, we have colored the poor black, and that will make it impossible to avoid the issue until it is resolved. Beyond that, if we have not defined all services as rights as some would wish, courts are becoming impatient with the failure to provide the services that *are* rights. They are beginning to insist that services intended to be made available should be made available.

On the other hand, profound forces will be arrayed against

universal services for children. Genuine costs, apparent more quickly than genuine benefits, will arouse resistance. Nor will we yield up superiority or contempt readily; quite often, they seem essential to our self-respect. The issue, therefore, is not programmatic but one of attitudinal and deep social change.

Yet, is it not useful to undertake programmatic steps that will permit or bring on social change in assimilable fashion? It is our children who are at stake, and the nation they will live in. Despite all the confusion and anxiety, we do love them.

NOTES

1. Lucille J. Grew and Ann W. Shyne, *Requests for Child Welfare Services* (New York: Child Welfare League of America, 1969), p. i. See also, Alfred J. Kahn, *Studies in Social Policy and Planning* (New York: Russell Sage Foundation, 1969), p. 253.
2. Henry S. Maas and Richard E. Engler, Jr., in collaboration with Zelma J. Felten and Margaret Purvine, *Children in Need of Parents* (New York: Columbia University Press, 1959), p. 352.
3. Charlotte Muller, "Socio-Economic Outcomes of Present Abortion Policy" (paper prepared for Workshop on Abortion, Bethesda, Md., December 15–16, 1969).
4. Leon Chestang, "The Dilemma of Biracial Adoption," *Social Work*, 17, no. 3 (May 1972).
5. David M. Kessner, *Infant Death: An Analysis by Maternal Risk and Health Care* (Washington, D.C.: National Academy of Sciences, 1973).
6. Rosemary Dinnage and M. L. Kellmer Pringle, *Foster Home Care, Facts and Fallacies, A Review of Research* (New York: Humanities Press, 1967); and Rosemary Dinnage and M. L. Kellmer Pringle, *Residential Child Care, Facts and Fallacies, A Review of Research* (New York: Humanities Press, 1967).
7. Dinnage and Pringle, *Foster Home Care, Facts and Fallacies*.
8. Martin Wolins, "Child Care in Cross-Cultural Perspective," (final report of a study supported by the National Institute of

Mental Health, the Ford Foundation, and the Institute of International Studies of the University of California, March 1969).

9. Martin Wolins and Mary Jane Owen, "Foster Care—Assumptions, Evidence, and Alternatives: An Exploratory Analysis" (paper prepared for the Joint Commission on Mental Health of Children, n.d.), p. 42.

10. Wolins and Owen, "Foster Care."

11. The term, converting private problems into public issues, and vice versa, is C. Wright Mills' explanation of the task of "the sociological imagination." See Mills, *The Sociological Imagination* (New York: Oxford University Press, 1959).

12. David Fanshel and Eugene B. Shinn, "Dollars and Sense in the Foster Care of Children: A Look at Cost Factors," Columbia University School of Social Work, 1972.

13. In *Regulating the Poor* (New York: Pantheon Books, 1971), Frances Fox Piven and Richard A. Cloward have made a similar argument. It is, indeed, the welfare program for children that they chiefly discuss. Piven and Cloward go further than the argument here. They regard AFDC not only as homeostatic, but as a device for regulating the threat of disorder in troubled times and, at other times, of forcing people into the labor market.

14. Mildred Arnold, "The Children's Titles in the Social Security Act: II. The Growth of Public Child Welfare Services," *Children*, 7, no. 4 (July–August 1960), 134.

15. During the 1960s, Alfred J. Kahn developed the concept of "social utilities" in an effort to encourage universal development of social services. Implicit is the view that programs such as child welfare had not developed universally because they were seen as necessary only for the maladjusted and the failures. If they could be seen as necessary for everybody, in a way analogous to water and power, universal development might be resumed. See Alfred J. Kahn, *Theory and Practice of Social Planning* (New York: Russell Sage Foundation, 1969), pp. 176–185.

16. Peter Townsend, "The Scope and Limitation of Means-Tested Social Services in Britain" (paper presented to the Manchester Statistical Society, February 29, 1972). See also Norman Mackenzie, ed., *Conviction* (London: McGibbon and Kee, 1959). For an account of the British debate on selectivity, see George Hoshino, "Britain's Debate on Universal or Selective Social Services: Lessons for America," *The Social Service Review*, 43, no. 3 (September 1969).

17. Robert J. Lampman, "Transfer and Redistribution as Social Process," in *Social Security in International Perspective*, ed. Shirley Jenkins (New York: Columbia University Press, 1969).
18. Alvin L. Schorr, *Explorations in Social Policy* (New York: Basic Books, 1968), p. 144.
19. For a selection of proposals, see Institute for Research on Poverty, *Welfare Reform: Problems and Solutions* (Madison: University of Wisconsin, n.d.); and The President's Commission on Income Maintenance Programs, *Background Papers* (Washington, D.C.: Government Printing Office, 1970).
20. Vincent H. Whitney, "Fertility Trends and Children's Allowance Programs," in *Children's Allowances and the Economic Welfare of Children*, ed. Eveline Burns, Citizen's Committee for Children of New York, 1968; and "Income and the Birth Rate," in Alvin L. Schorr, *Poor Kids* (New York: Basic Books, 1966), Chapter 5.
21. 92d Cong., 2d sess., H.R. 17196, A bill to amend the Social Security Act to provide for a system of children's allowances, and for other purposes. By Mr. Fraser (Minn.), Ms. Abzug (N.Y.), Mr. Badillo (N.Y.), Mr. Collins (Ill.), Mr. Conyers (Mich.), and Mr. Diggs (Mich.).
22. For an analysis of the impact of children's allowances on poverty and moderate incomes, see Vera Shlakman, *Children's Allowances* (New York: Citizen's Committee for Children, 1970); and Schorr, *Poor Kids*.
23. *Family Allowances and Social Security, Lady Rhys-Williams' Scheme* (London: Liberal Publication Dept., 1944).
24. First to write about the concept in the United States was Professor Earl R. Rolph; the intellectual father of Senator McGovern's scheme was Professor James Tobin. See Earl R. Rolph, "A Credit Income Tax," *Industrial Relations*, 6, no. 2 (February 1967).
25. *Proposals for a Tax-Credit System*, Command 5116, Her Majesty's Stationery Office, London.
26. Subcommittee on Fiscal Policy, Joint Economic Committee of Congress, paper no. 1, "Public Income Transfer Programs: The Incidence of Multiple Benefits and the Issues Raised by Their Receipt," and paper no. 4, "Income Transfer Programs: How They Tax the Poor" (Washington, D.C.: Government Printing Office, 1972).
27. See David G. Gil, *Unravelling Social Policy—Theory, Analysis, and Political Action Toward Social Equality* (Cambridge, Mass.: Schenkman Publishing Co., 1972); David G. Gil, "Mothers' Wages, An Alternative Attack on Poverty," *Social*

Work Practice, 1969 (New York: Columbia University Press, 1969); and "Federal Work Strategies," in *Work in America,* Report of a Special Task Force to the Secretary of Health, Education, and Welfare, December 1972. Processed.

28. See "Fatherless Child Insurance," in Schorr, *Poor Kids,* Chapter 7.
29. Julius Richmond, "Child Health in America: Toward a National Public Policy" (paper prepared for the National Research Council, June 1972), pp. 48, 51.
30. Richard M. Titmuss, *Commitment to Welfare* (London: George Allen and Unwin, 1968) pp. 113–114.

INDEX

Abbott, Grace, 19
abortion: and poor families, 187, 188
accountability: in foster care, 46
Addams, Jane, 169
Ad Hoc Committee on Foster Care of Children (New York State Board of Social Welfare), 46, 47
adolescent children: boarding schools for, 66
adoption, 13–14, 187–188; interracial, 188; placement, 40
Advisory Council on Public Welfare, 122
Advisory Council on Social Security, 200
aged, 62, 196; spending per capita on, xi
Aid to Families with Dependent Children (AFDC), 11, 28, 92, 100, 101, 102, 113–114, 116–117, 194, 195, 198, 199; "absent parent" provision, 135; benefits, 121–123; eligibility for, 118–121; and poor families, 133–134; racial bias, 125; social policy for children, 135–138; social services, 126–132; and substandard housing, 124–125
Aid to the Blind (AB), 115
Aid to the Permanently and Totally Disabled (APTD), 115
almshouses, 69
American Academy of Pediatrics, 154, 156–157
American Indian children: and AFDC, 114; boarding schools for, 60, 61, 67, 72, 76; "civilizing" of,

66–67; infant mortality rate, 152
apprentices: children as, 6–7

Bennett, Wallace F., 205
binding out: practice of, 7
birth rate: and day care, 96
births: out-of-wedlock, 13–14; unwanted, 188
black children, 61; and adoption, 13–14; and AFDC, 114; and day care, 15; and foster care, 32; length of foster placement, 38; needy, 3; and slavery, 8; and voluntary agencies, 18
black families: and AFDC, 125; and family day care, 103; and public assistance, 29, 119
blue-collar workers: and family day care, 103
boarding-out system, 31–32
boarding schools: vs. child welfare institutions, 70–71, 74, 82; for Indian Children, 60, 61, 67, 72, 76; private, 55–56, 60, 64, 68, 72, 73, 76
Brace, Charles Loring, 30
Bremner, Robert H., 67
Briar, Scott, 37
busing, xii, 197
Byrnes, John W., 205

Canada: children's allowances in, 201
cash benefit schemes, 113, 118, 127
Chapman, Judith E., 100
child abuse, xii; and family income, 12; among nonpoor, 34